AFTER THE APPLE

AFTER

THE

APPLE

WOMEN IN THE BIBLE

Timeless Stories of Love, Lust, and Longing

NAOMI HARRIS ROSENBLATT

MIRAMAX BOOKS

ISBN 0-7868-6908-9

To my husband, Peter;

To my children,

Therese, Marshall, Daniel, Laura and David; and to my grandchildren,

Zachary, Samuel, Jacob, Abigail and Benjamin

CONTENTS

INTRODUCTION

✦

M Y LOVE AFFAIR WITH THE Hebrew Bible began in first grade at the Reali School in Haifa, Israel, when I was six. Even as a child, I sensed that if I studied this one Book thoroughly, I would understand all there is to know about the adult world without ever leaving my neighborhood. Since then, I have viewed life and people through the lens of the biblical stories. As I grow older, I never tire of returning to these familiar human dramas, mining them for fresh insights and spiritual nourishment.

Soon after I began my biblical studies, I asked my father a question I desperately wanted him to answer: "Daddy, do you believe in God?"

My nonobservant father was well versed in the Bible and I knew he would answer me honestly. A Scottish Jew of few words, he would invariably reply "I don't know." Looking back, I see that the Second World War was raging at the time and his faith in a benevolent God was being tested.

An art critic, my father followed a similar policy at exhibits. I would plead, "Which is your favorite painting?" but he never gave me a direct answer.

Over the years I came to understand that he wanted me to search for my own answers—for that I am grateful.

My mother, a nonpracticing lawyer from a Canadian Jewish family, was always entranced by the complexities of human nature. We spent hours together discussing the marital or romantic relationships of our neighbors, family, and friends. When I would return from school and recount details about Bible stories I found particularly moving, she was a reliable captive audience. Shaking her head in amazement, she would murmur, "What wisdom, what wisdom;" a response that only confirmed my belief that this Book held the clues to understanding life. When on one of our long walks we would encounter a child crippled by polio, my mother would lament her inability to possess a deeper faith. I could not bear seeing her unhappy. My answer was always the same, that the fact that she talked so much about it was in itself an act of faith, that God was not interested in blind faith, that her musings bespoke her compassion and caring—and that that genuinely served God's purpose.

In school I continued studying the Bible until the age of eighteen, seeking a deeper level every year. Dr. Josef Schechter, my rotund high school teacher and a renowned biblical scholar, would dart around the room enthusiastically waving a small Bible, prodding us to speculate, debate and arrive at a higher level of understanding. His passion for the Book was contagious. He imprinted on our minds the rabbinical wisdom that each word of the biblical narrative has seventy possible interpretations. He (like my father) offered no definitive answers but encouraged us to develop our own ideas and insights.

Our school took us on numerous hikes and excursions around the country. We visited Beersheba, where four thousand years ago Sarah and Abraham, the founding pioneers of a new faith, waited for the birth of the child promised by God. We walked on the road where Rachel, Jacob's beloved wife, died giving birth to Benjamin. We hiked in the desert around Ein Gedi, on the shore of the Dead Sea, where the young David fled to hide from King Saul. We looked down from the hilltops of Jerusalem, where King David caught sight of the beautiful Bathsheba bathing on the low, flat roof of her house. Girls and boys packed into an open truck, we drove south along the Mediterranean coast where the mighty Samson searched for the love of Philistine women and stumbled upon his nemesis, Delilah.

In school we began each class by reading aloud the chapter we were to study that day. When we became teenagers, we studied the more difficult material—Isaiah, Jeremiah, Amos, and other prophets—becoming familiar with their pleas and demands for compassion and social justice, with their anger at Israel's sins and the accompanying message of healing and redemption. We were not required to memorize the words, but sentences and entire passages stayed with us for life because of the sheer beauty of the language.

We needed no translation because the Bible was written in Hebrew, our mother tongue. The language connected us to our distant but very real past. It seemed that the two millennia when our more recent ancestors had sojourned in Europe—including the golden age in Spain, the oppression in Europe—spoke to us less vividly than this ancient text. I was reared during World War II and the postwar era, and many of my European neighbors were refugees with concentration camp numbers tattooed on their arms. I was often invited for an afternoon to join one or another of them on their balconies to enjoy a rich chocolate torte. I listened and absorbed their stories of escape, heart-wrenching losses, and ultimate survival. Alone in bed at night, I would imagine how I would have handled losing my parents while trying to escape across hostile borders, and then I would fall asleep sobbing into my pillow. But still the fifteen hundred years of biblical history claimed precedence. The text was ours. It was an important part of who we were.

The unsentimental realism of the Hebrew Bible helped us deal with our personal issues as well as the complex predicaments we faced in our country. There were political realities beyond our control but the biblical message was both hopeful and empowering, especially when the situation was difficult. We knew that we had to rise to the needs of the hour and never give up. Our country was tiny and young and we knew that her survival depended solely on us. Even as teenagers we worked in summer camps helping to settle new immigrants, or we worked in agricultural communities. The work we did was real and made a difference. The adults treated us with respect. All of these circumstances developed our self-confidence, a sense of responsibility and self-reliance.

The journey that began during childhood Bible study with its accompanying emphasis on interpretation and reinterpretation eventually led me to my work as a psychotherapist. Now, years later,

as a mature woman—a wife, a parent, a teacher, and a therapist—
I have become aware how profoundly the stories of the women of
the Hebrew Bible informed my point of view. The biblical stories
deal with provocative material: sexuality, consolation of a mother's
grief over the loss of a child, a wife yearning for the unreciprocated
love of her husband or the unabashed delight of a couple in their
mutual passion. Thus the groundwork had been laid for discussing
intimate issues with my patients; I found it so natural.

Equally significant, I grew to appreciate my patients' resilience because I had learned how that quality was indispensable in
the stories of the ancient women I so admired. Their life stories
taught me the importance of stressing the need for a personal sense
of identity, a strong core of spiritual beliefs and values. Like the
mothers in the book of Genesis, I too am concerned with transmitting to my children a well-defined set of values and knowledge of
their legacy, tools they will carry with them into the future.

I am grateful for the Bible's candor in presenting humanity with
heroics accompanied by frailties and imperfections. By portraying
life as it is, with all its contradictions and complexities, the Bible has
guided me along the path of compassion, empathy, and understanding of others. I learned about the dangers of lust from David and
Bathsheba, about pain and jealousy from Sarah, about love and loyalty
from Ruth and Naomi, about courage and guile from Esther, about
tenacity and endurance from Leah. The stories are permeated with
a sense of spiritual urgency: at the moment of crisis, each heroine is
conscious of being in the presence of God, aware that whatever
choice she makes will have a profound impact exceeding the bounds
of her own life, and that her responsibilities extend to her family, her
people, and their spiritual identity and, indeed, their very survival.

Ever since I was very young, I have wanted to be Rebecca: to look and walk like her when returning from the well, head held high, with a jug of water hoisted on one shoulder. I too wanted to be hospitable and generous. However, my focus expanded when I reread her story as I conducted a Bible class for ten to fifteen women in Washington for over twenty years. We met every Friday morning over a steaming pot of tea around my dining room table.

During one of our lively discussions I found myself identifying with what the young Rebecca must have felt upon leaving her mother, father, and country to start her married life with a stranger in a strange land—her longings, hopes, excitement, guilt. The courage of the mature Rebecca in sending off her younger son Jacob to a faraway place reminded me of my parents' courage in permitting me to fly the nest when I was very young to join my equally young husband in an unfamiliar land. Like Rebecca, I felt there was no room for self-pity. There was a marriage to pay attention to and children to bring up. Yet I wondered to whom she poured out her heart. How lonely and homesick she must have felt despite her husband Isaac's fidelity and love for her. Denial and suppression were an essential coping mechanism in my early years in America. The more I revisited Rebecca's story, the more its relevance to my life struck me. Knowing that I was not alone in this predicament was immensely comforting to me.

I also ran a Bible class on Capitol Hill with senators and spouses of different faiths and political parties. It is gratifying to see these powerful leaders, like so many before them, turn for wisdom and an hour of introspection to an ancient book of an ancient people. A discussion of David's adulterous relationship with Bathsheba, wife of Uriah, coincided with the Monica Lewinsky affair. A spirited, frank debate ensued on the extent to which the personal life of a leader impacts the quality of his or her governance, as well as on the conflicts between sexual privacy and family values, and the troubling symbiosis of power and sex. Bathsheba's affair with the king offered the group a safe place in which to discuss issues of power, temptation, and moral responsibilities as these related to their personal lives.

A number of women in my Friday morning group felt deep sympathy for Bathsheba's loneliness. One woman after another argued that Bathsheba's husband, an army officer, was gone for long stretches of time and seemed impervious to the toll it was taking on their relationship. The consensus was that Bathsheba was ripe for an affair: she does, after all, take baths on a low-lying roof in full view of the king's house. From the spare biblical account, conversation turned to the importance of taking care of couplehood and nurturing the emotional and sexual bonds between husband and wife, especially now, when our days are frantic and frequent travel is an integral part of our lives. The group concluded that couplehood must become a conscious priority between mates.

At one point the Senate group was analyzing the sexual tension, the pain, and the suffering in Abraham's household when the infertile Sarah arranged for her husband to beget a child with a surrogate mother. A senator considered distant and impersonal astonished the group by vehemently declaring that regardless of a man's feelings for "the other woman," the wife's interests must come first. The oldest senator by far in the group was deeply concerned with the sibling rivalry so central to the Genesis saga. A Southerner, he used the Civil War as a prime example of the tragic price that sibling rivalry exacts.

Reading the Bible in a group is wonderfully beneficial and enjoyable, with each member contributing insights and interpretations based on diverse life experiences and personal needs guided, however, at the end of the day, by specific values and ethics. The Bible has never failed to be inspiring. I believe that is so because this ancient book presents life as untidy and riddled with contradictions yet at the same time expects all of us to seek the spiritual and moral high ground. This recognition of an earthy humanity with its frailties, taken together with a demand for betterment is what enables the Bible to speak to each of us directly. The Bible's message is of tough love and its power is uncanny.

For many reasons, beginning with my upbringing and continuing through my professional life I have never viewed the Bible as a religious or historical document alone. Rather, I have seen it as a series of living dramas of my forebears. Since I am a woman, the women in the Bible especially appeal to me. The overwhelmingly difficult circumstances they faced with resolve and ingenuity continue as issues for women today: how to communicate with a mate and male authority figures, conception and infertility and childrearing.

Legally, ancient Hebrew women were strictly subordinate to the male heads of the household, first as daughters to their fathers, then as wives to their husbands. Sons inherited their father's property, and when they married, they became the heads of their own families. With marriage, a woman joined her husband's family and passed from the authority of her father to that of her husband.

When revisiting and reexamining the Bible's treatment of women, I was surprised by what I found. I did not find women to be groveling servants or blindly obedient wives. They question the patriarchs. They use their power as women to subvert, to seduce, to trick their men. They use their feminine intelligence to challenge patriarchal authority when it stands in the way of their own, their family's, and their people's survival. Most surprisingly, as the stories attest, these courageous, proactive women are not punished, but are instead rewarded for their boldness. The women's commitment to transmitting the Covenant and the blessings to the next generation is indispensable. The biblical scribes, presumably mostly men, are sympathetic to the women's predicaments and, convinced of their importance, recorded in detail the risks they took, their heroism, and their resourcefulness.

When I reread the stories of women of the Hebrew Bible, I feel at one with them. I feel related to them. And now, many years after my first youthful readings, I still remember their trials and their triumphs and am touched by their strength and faith. When I read the Bible, I learn to be more compassionate and understanding, and less judgmental, to wonder and take delight in whatever inspired the women's actions, to understand that we are part of a long chain of humanity. The stories give me support and succor.

THIS BOOK FOLLOWS THE ANCIENT Jewish tradition of midrash; the constant reinterpretation of the Bible stories to derive from them new ethical and spiritual applications to meet the issues and concerns of succeeding generations. Unlike novels, the Bible does not disclose the feelings, motivations, and thoughts of the characters. It usually presents actions without much comment. It also highlights certain incidents with particular detail, repeats others, and skips over great chunks of time. The Bible's gaps, repetitions, and terse, laconic literary style invite readers to construct their own perspectives and interpretations, to search for motives and to make the stories applicable to their own lives and situations. My interpretation and perspective are the product of years of study, teaching, and writing on biblical subjects, my experience as a psychotherapist, and above all my accumulated personal life experiences.

My mission and my passion is to extricate the women's voices from a male-centered narrative. However, it is important to recall the words of Thomas Babington Macaulay, who said, "We ought not to try the men of one age by the standard of another."

I view the women of the Bible through a contemporary lens, but I never ignore the context of their day-to-day lives: a patriarchal and polygamous society, a short life span, no birth control, and a fifty percent infant mortality at minimum. However constrained their lives might have been, however, they were fiercely aware that their actions mattered not only to themselves but to generations to come.

Finally, I urge my readers to follow the advice of Martin Buber, the great philosopher and theologian: "Read the Bible as though it were something entirely unfamiliar, as though it had not been set before you ready made. . . . Let whatever may happen occur between yourself and it. You do not know which of its sayings and images will overwhelm you . . . hold yourself open."

NOTE: THE TRANSLATION OF THE Hebrew Bible used in this book is primarily that of the Jewish Publication Society, 1985, but wherever considerations of accuracy require I have felt free to use other translations or to supply my own.

AFTER THE APPLE

ONE

EVE:

THE FIRST REBEL

I T ALL STARTED WITH EVE, the mother of us all. The story of the first humans, Eve and Adam, opens the Bible with a tangle of loneliness, companionship, desire, and love. It tells how woman, made in the Creator's image, gives up a life of ease in an idyllic setting, along with the promise of immortality, and in its stead chooses to pursue wisdom and intimacy with her man. Locked within the story of the first couple is a matrix for all the male/female partnerships that follow. Eve is the prototype for the other women in the book. She is the one who takes risks to create life. She generates the future.

The invisible Mover behind the scenes is an all-knowing, loving

God who sets all the elements in place: a man, a woman, the lush garden, the talking serpent, the fruit-bearing trees. In the story the Creator teaches us about the exercise of free will, the need to be responsible for the consequences of our actions, and the bumpy road to growing up and leaving home.

"God created man in His image, in the image of God He created him; male and female He created them." Familiar translations of the Hebrew treat both God and Adam as male. In fact, however, we don't know what the image of God is: God may be male, female, androgynous, or have no gender whatsoever. The genius of the biblical God is that He transcends definition—a revolutionary departure from the way idols were conceived at the time. In Hebrew the word for the first human, *Adam*, is in fact a generic term for "human being" and is thus neither masculine nor feminine. In English the word *man* is traditionally used to encompass all mankind, both male and female. The Bible and the English translations then go on to specify that "male and female He created them."

The setting is idyllic. I envision Adam enjoying the company of playful animals. Wonder fills his soul as he watches birds soaring across the sky. He runs with the beasts, climbs tall trees, and skips flat stones on the river's surface. The Garden of Eden is an ideal playground; a place of innocence where life is beautiful, easy, and safe, lacking all challenges. The mythologies of many cultures refer to such a place in prehistorical times. The prevalence of this concept suggests a universal nostalgia for an idealized childhood.

In this beautiful and abundant setting, however, "no fitting helper for Adam was found," because humankind is unique among God's creatures, created in the likeness of God's own image. Adam can find no other creature that walks upright and is able to contemplate both the heavens above and the earth below. No other living being cries or laughs like him. No other creature even uses facial expressions to indicate emotion or meaning or ideas the way he does. More significantly, no other creature talks. Adam the human is unique among the creatures because he has been granted the gift of language. He gives names to the animals in the Garden of Eden and can express amazement and gratitude with words. But to whom? The human Adam has no one with whom to use words, communicate feelings, or exchange ideas.

Surveying all He has created, God observes with compassion the loneliness of the human being among the animals. He says, "It is not good for Adam to be alone; I will make a fitting helper for him." The first human emotion the Bible grapples with is loneliness.

The Creator responds quickly, first anesthetizing Adam and then performing surgery: "So the Lord God cast a deep sleep upon the man; and, while he slept, He took one of his ribs and closed up the flesh at that spot. And the Lord God fashioned the rib that He had taken from the man into a woman."

Adam is now unquestionably male and Eve is his female counterpart. Is God aware of the energy He is unleashing by separating the human into man and woman? Or has woman been part of His secret plan all along?

The Hebrew word *tzela* is customarily translated as "rib," but another of its meanings is "side"—as in the side of a ship or a house, or an essential structural component of the whole. The term suggests that if you remove the "side," the structure falls apart. That the first woman is made from the first human's "side," from very close to his heart, tells us that man and woman are two halves of a once-intact whole. On the one hand man now has a separate companion to share his life with and from whom he can gain a different perspective. On the other hand after they are separated each half pursues the other yearning to become one again. As the Bible puts it in words that leap the confines of time and space: "Hence a man leaves his father and mother and clings to his wife, so that they become one flesh." With this passage, the Bible indicates the potential for man and woman when they join together in mind, heart, and body to pursue a single goal, most fruitfully expressed over time as family and offspring.

God did not consult man about the creation of woman. Adam did not ask for a companion, was not even aware of the deficiency in his life, did not have the imagination to dream up the possibility that he might have a companion like him and yet very different. Woman, like man, is entirely the Creator's idea. Woman owes man nothing for her creation. Both are created in God's image, which means they have free choice, and both are thus morally and spiritually equal in His eyes. (Most of the world, now as then, has yet to catch up with this fact.)

The Creator "brought her to the man," and He presents her with a courteous flourish. Man is instantly moved to poetry: "This one at last / Is bone of my bones / And flesh of my flesh." Once he sees her, "at last," he knows what he has been missing.

Now man has a "fitting companion," different but equal, who stands upright like him and laughs and cries and talks like him. Both are naked but neither is ashamed. They are as innocent as infants romping at the beach.

The story links the ideas of speech and human companionship. Adam can talk to the animals and give them names but they cannot talk back to him. Speech (like the telephone) is valuable only when others have use of it as well. In Genesis, the story first tells us that God grants Adam, out of all His creatures, the unique gift of language. Only afterwards does God declare His compassion for the human's loneliness and the need for a fit companion equal to him. It is precisely God's gift of speech that makes man—in contrast to the animal kingdom—so conscious of his solitude when he lacks a companion of his own kind.

The Bible introduces the idea of the need for companionship before it even mentions sexuality and procreation. In my professional experience, only after the male and the female can articulate their separateness and uniqueness are they equipped to express their mutual need and respect for each other and affirm their interdependence. Spouses in a healthy, supportive relationship praise and appreciate the strengths and values of their mates, and they also feel secure in communicating decisions and behaviors that the other spouse may consider unacceptable.

By introducing the need for companionship first, the Bible's point is that the companionship we offer our mates is the most enduring and rare gift we can bring to an intimate relationship. Sharing our sorrows and joys, exchanging ideas about a good book or movie and praying together; all that is facilitated by speech. Sexual desire—although indispensable—may ebb and flow, but the human desire and need for companionship is constant. Companionship in a strong, enduring human relationship requires attention and awareness from both parties. The longer the relationship endures, the more we become aware of how the long years build up trust and tenderness that cannot be duplicated. One rabbinical commentary suggests that woman was created second so that man could experience loneliness and more fully appreciate his partner. Another opines that is Adam named the animals as they passed by him in pairs he commented "Everything has its partner, but I have no partner."

Another point the Bible suggests is that monogamy is more rewarding than polygamy. God creates one, not multiple, companions for Adam. Anthropologists tell us that men are generally polygamously inclined in consequence of a genetic drive to procreate whenever the opportunity arises. Yet it seems to me that by creating just one woman for the sole man the story is telling us that monogamy is the preferred state and that men need to curb, tame, and control their instinctive sexual drive. Monogamous marriage has been referred to by the psychologist Ned Gaylin as "the institution for civilizing" sexuality.

The Bible suggests that human beings are most nurtured by deep and lasting emotional relationships and the more we put into a relationship the more we get out of it. Multiple or serial relationships dilute the intensity that a monogamous relationship can develop because it concentrates the emotional, sexual, and intellectual aspects of human beings into a single focus. Each time we read of a biblical polygamous family, we read of suffering and pain.

IN THE TREE-FILLED GARDEN of Eden, God designates one tree off limits and warns man never to touch its fruit on pain of death. The forbidden fruit is that of the tree of knowledge of good and evil. The Hebrew word for knowledge, *da'at*, means sexual knowledge. "To know" is the biblical verb which implies more than the sexual act alone. It is an elegant euphemism for the intimate and sensitive understanding that evolves over time within a sexual relationship.

Lurking about the forbidden tree is a serpent, "the shrewdest of all the wild beasts." Sidling up to the woman, it asks if God really forbade eating fruit from the trees of the garden. She corrects the serpent: "God allows the eating of the fruits of all trees, except for the one in the middle of the garden." She recites God's edict (presumably told to her by Adam): "You shall not eat of it or touch it, lest you die."

The serpent tells the woman: "You are not going to die, but God knows that as soon as you eat of it your eyes will be opened and you will be like divine beings who know good and evil."

The serpent, a phallic symbol and fertility idol in cultures across the world, is a reflection of the sexual yearnings stirring in the woman's body and soul. As the two of them carry on the first conversation recorded in the Bible chronicles, the serpent cunningly addresses the woman's unconscious and casts doubts.

Woman is not easily swayed. She is not rash; she takes her time and deliberates; she is aware that the punishment for disobedience to God will be severe. The Bible indicates that time elapses between the serpent's prodding and woman's decision to take from the tree: she is alone when the serpent works to persuade her, but then she is with Adam when she finally reaches for the fruit.

"When the woman saw that the tree was good for eating and a delight to the eyes, and that the tree was desirable as a source of wisdom, she took the fruit and ate. Then she gave some to her husband, and he ate."

Eve deliberates before eating the forbidden fruit but Adam devours it without hesitation and without questioning the consequences. We may assume he feels happy and appreciated.

The fruit has an instantaneous effect: "Then the eyes of both of them were opened and they perceived that they were naked; and they sewed together fig leaves" to cover their private parts. Before eating the fruit of the forbidden tree, they were unconcerned with privacy; they had nothing to hide either from their Creator or from each other. But after eating the fruit, for the first time they become self-conscious, aware of being looked at, and ashamed in front of each other. Privacy thus becomes part of human sexuality.

The repast of fruit in the garden is a defining moment in the human saga. Soon the first couple's repertory of emotions expands to include shame, guilt, and desire. Man and woman, like all the human beings who will follow them, begin the awkward and painful transition from the innocence of childhood to sexual awareness, awakening, experience, and accountability. It is the beginning of puberty—and maturation. Woman's sexual awakening goes hand in hand with the life force, the drive to procreate. She *must* attract the man to her because she cannot conceive on her own. As the Bible suggests, man and woman must cooperate to provide the human infant with the love, nourishment, and safety it requires to grow and thrive. No other new life is so helpless for so long as that of the human infant.

GOD CREATED HUMANS WITH THE power of free will—in contrast to animals, all of whom are driven by instinct. He knows that woman will be the first to take advantage of His gift and be drawn to the forbidden tree. In accord with His grand scheme, Eve is biologically, genetically, and mentally designed to perpetuate the species. Like every woman after her, she is born with all the eggs she will need for every child she will ever bear.

Embedded in this charming allegory of sexual awakening is

the gap between the female and male sexual response. Woman's arousal is gradual and internal, enlisting all her senses, emotions, and imagination, as described in Eve's deliberations before tasting the forbidden fruit. We imagine her eyes and senses trained on the fruit and the process she goes through before she is convinced to take the ultimate step. "And when the woman saw that the tree was good for food and that it was a delight to the eye, and that the tree was to be desired to make one wise, she took of its fruit and did eat," the Bible says. The procreative drive has now been awakened within her and overwhelms all other considerations. For the woman, the consequences of a sexual relationship can be much more serious than for the man. She is the one who becomes pregnant, and for nine months. Her decision is therefore more deliberate and takes more time than the man's.

Eve reaches out to Adam, holding the fruit (the shape of which suggests fertility, the female breast). In contrast to the female, the male is immediately susceptible to any sexual invitation, is instantly responsive. Observing the unthinking ease with which man accepts the forbidden fruit from her hand, woman has already learned that man succumbs easily to sexual temptation. The female ignites the flame of his desire by her mere presence or through the subtlest of means—a signature perfume, a smile, flattery, the offering of an apple—and the male is immediately seduced. This theme of man's instant responsiveness runs through the Bible, which repeatedly depicts women in desperate circumstances (Tamar the daughter-in-law of Judah is an example, as is Ruth) successfully relying on the male's vulnerability to sexual seduction.

The biblical text gives no indication that man gives the tree of knowledge so much as a second thought. He is just as content to eat the fruit from the other trees and avoid the one tree that God forbade him. He is both passive and incurious.

Hearing God moving about in the garden, man and woman panic and hide, aware of their disobedience and that there will be consequences. God calls out to man, "Where are you?" He replies, "I was afraid because I was naked, so I hid."

God asks, "Who told you that you were naked? Did you eat of the tree from which I forbade you to eat?"

Man's immediate defense is to blame the woman as well as God: "The woman You put at my side—she gave me of the tree, and I ate."

God then turns to woman: "What is this you have done!"

She replies, "The serpent duped me, and I ate."

Both man and woman shirk their own responsibility by blaming someone else. Man could have chosen to protect woman, who has just fed him and given him pleasure. He could have been truthful and mentioned that she did not force him to partake of the forbidden fruit. Woman could have explained that she chose to trade immortality in the Garden of Eden for knowledge and wisdom. Like man, however, she is fearful, and she blames the serpent, disavowing any accountability for her action.

It is easier to blame others for our actions, but scapegoating has been a constant issue in human society. It allows both societies and individuals to ignore their own choices and decisions and to blame others for their problems. Scapegoating leads to terrible cruelty and murder, which leads to more problems because the original problems are never faced and dealt with. In the short term, it may keep the peace, but in the long term, it always fails.

Both man and woman also feel scared and guilty. A uniquely

human trait, guilt is indispensable to developing self-awareness and a conscience. Guilt spurs us to improve ourselves, to try harder to do the right thing.

Accepting responsibility is the mature choice that leads to emotional growth. We need to summon up the courage and humility to blame ourselves and accept blame from others, often publicly, for our behavior. When we accept responsibility, we don't blame others for decisions we made, and we recognize and acknowledge how our actions affect other people. Once we accept blame, we accept the consequences. This often means accepting punishment, whether punishment takes the form of a curfew, the loss of driving privileges, or a jail sentence.

Taking responsibility for our imperfections is empowering, because blaming someone else for our actions necessarily assumes that we are victims who are acted upon. Acknowledging that everything we do matters focuses on the adult in us rather than the child. There must follow a behavioral change or at least a genuine effort; words alone are empty.

Young children are not responsible for their actions because they have no understanding of the consequences of their actions. Only people who are old enough to have good judgment, "to know better," and can act independently without being coerced, are held responsible for what they do.

Eating the forbidden fruit of the tree of knowledge of good and evil is the first independent act by the human beings in the Garden of Eden. Adam and Eve cannot be said to have been fully aware of the extent of their transgression because they did not yet have knowledge of good and evil. They do, however, know that God has told them explicitly not to eat of that tree. In that respect, they are like children, who may understand that certain behavior is expected but do not fully understand why.

Like any concerned parent, God wants His children to grow up and learn to accept responsibility for their actions, however painful that may be for them, and for Him. Indeed, God has lovingly provided all of the arrangements in the garden—a secure life, the edict against one tree; but also human capacity for free choice that will cause Adam and Eve to grow and mature. He, the all-seeing Creator, knows perfectly well where the humans are in the garden, but He asks His question, "Where are you?" to draw the story out of them and begin the process of moral awareness and development.

God becomes angry not so much at the act of disobedience but at Adam and Eve's avoidance of responsibility and their insistence on blaming others. Significantly, the word *sin* is not introduced in the Bible until later, when Cain murders his brother, Abel. It seems that Adam and Eve's worst transgression is their scapegoating, and the couple's moral life will finally begin when they can acknowledge having done wrong.

Seductive and aggressive, a narcissist, the serpent is deemed the archvillain of the story. It proves more articulate than man, and its courtship of woman is as ardent as it is cunning. It is involved with the woman strictly for its own pleasure and gratification. The serpent derives perverse excitement from successfully tempting Eve. It is a villain because of the baseness of its motives, not because of the act it encourages. The serpent began its existence standing erect, an image that suggests sexual enticement, and according to rabbinical tradition, that is how it spoke to the woman. God disapproves of this narcissism and severely punishes the serpent. No wonder we call a sneaky, selfish person "a snake"!

God tells the serpent, "Because you did this, more cursed shall you
be than all the cattle and all the wild beasts: On your belly shall
you crawl and dirt shall you eat all the days of your life. I will put
enmity between you and the woman, and between your offspring and
hers; they shall strike at your head and you shall strike at their
heel."

God's first punishment reduces the offending serpent's entire
species to the humiliation of crawling and eating dirt. From that
time on, human beings must guard against the serpent as it slithers
beneath rocks and into vegetation, hissing and creeping on its belly,
ready for ambush.

Having meted out His sternest punishment, God then turns to
woman: "I will make most severe your pain in childbearing; in pain
shall you bear children; yet your urge shall be for your husband and
he shall rule over you."

Even with modern medicine, giving birth is not free of pain
or risk. After birth, however, a protective amnesia sets in and the
life force within the mother prevails. Memory of the pain recedes
and the woman once again desires sexual union with her partner
and looks forward to the new life it promises. That too is part of
God's grand design, because God and humans want and need life to
continue through generations. The suppression of the memory of
pain in childbirth is part of a fundamental optimism about the future, about hope and a new beginning. It represents a victory over
loss and death.

The verse "he shall rule over you" describes male/female relations in ancient times and in parts of the world today. Even today in

many countries birth control is nonexistent and a woman may carry one child in her belly and one at her breast while her other children are tugging at her skirts. Mother and children are entirely dependent upon the husband's protection. Moreover, since physical strength is essential for survival in the harsh conditions of an agricultural society, men often use their overwhelming physical strength to subjugate and abuse women. The biblical text, however, makes another point. The Hebrew word for "rule," *limshol* shares a root with *moshel*, a responsible ruler or governor who takes care of his family—not a tyrant.

Next, God addresses man: "Because you did as your wife said and ate of the tree about which I commanded you, 'You shall not eat of it,'

> *cursed be the ground because of you; by toil shall you eat of it all the days of your life: Thorns and thistles shall it sprout for you. But your food shall be the grasses of the field; by the sweat of your brow shall you get bread to eat, until you return to the ground—for from it you were taken. For dust you are, and to dust you shall return."*

Significantly, God's edict that man must till the soil to bring forth food follows immediately after His pronouncement on woman's role, linking their roles together as complementary. It is clear that Adam and Eve's relationship is about collaboration, not subjugation.

Woman is to bring forth life with pain, but she will also derive satisfaction from watching her offspring grow up and mature. Man is to eke out a living from the soil by the sweat of his brow, but his labor will also enable him to feed his family with pride and a sense of accomplishment. Man and woman bear the burdens and joys of adult life equally and together; these are the consequences of their having eaten fruit from the tree of knowledge of good and evil, of sexual knowledge in its broadest sense. The male/female relationship in Genesis is not about dominance and submission but rather about interdependence and cooperation.

The humans' reactions to God's judgments go unrecorded. God's devastating final punishment—"For dust you are, and to dust you shall return"—is followed by an apparent nonsequitur: "the man named his wife Eve [*Hava* in Hebrew], because she was the mother of all the living." This name highlights Eve as the archetype for all women, whose unique role is to give life. It is the first of rare husband-to-wife compliments in the Bible; it is also hardly the contrite admission of guilt that might be expected in response to God's stern edicts. Instead, man and woman turn to each other and participate in the significant ritual act of giving a name—and what a name!—which suggests Adam's appreciative support for his wife's action. He has stopped blaming her.

The next sentence exemplifies God's compassion and mercy. He upgrades the fig leaves they wear to "garments of skins for Adam and his wife." His gift of clothing protects His children from the elements outside the garden. The garments also portend the beginnings of aesthetic appreciation and with it, civilization.

Adam and Eve's expulsion from the Garden of Eden is necessitated by a second tree in the garden, one previously mentioned but playing no part in the story thus far. God, mysteriously using the royal *we*, observes: "Now that man has become like one of us, what if he should stretch out his hand and take also from the tree of life and eat, and live forever!" Now that man has breached the previous demarcation by gaining knowledge of good and evil, the Creator is determined to draw a line between the human and the divine; human beings are henceforth destined to live as mortals. God not only banishes Adam "to till the soil from which he was taken," but also we are told that He "drove the man out, and stationed east of the Garden of Eden the cherubim and the fiery ever-turning sword, to guard the way to the tree of life."

Eve and Adam leave their Father's protective abode, as children must. God knows it is time for them to face life as adults in an imperfect world. The heartbroken Parent appoints a guard at the garden's gate to prevent Eve and Adam from regressing to a childhood devoid of adult responsibilities, but also to prevent Himself from softening and allowing them to return. All humans must go through this process of leaving home, starting with birth. Each must leave a childhood characterized by trust, security, and unconditional love and go beyond the boundaries of home. One demarcation is sexual initiation. Once this occurs, there can be no pretense at former innocence. There is no turning back.

The Garden of Eden offers a life that is comfortable and risk free. Food is abundant and available without toil. There are no wild beasts threatening harm. Immortality seems within reach. Yet Eve rejects the stultifying monotony of her perfect, paradisiacal life. As she gazes at the forbidden tree of knowledge, she seems to ask, What good is life without the wisdom that arises from experience? Passing by the tree of life she might muse, Of what use is immortality without knowledge or growth? Eve wrestles with humanity's first moral dilemma and takes the first moral action recorded in the Bible when she crosses the limit set by the all-knowing God.

The reader sees Eve and Adam leaving the Garden of Eden full of optimism. Our hearts go out to the naïve young couple walking hand in hand, confident about the future and ready to take on its endless unknowns.

They are not at all the tearful, dejected couple portrayed in Renaissance art, expelled by a furious Father. The first thing they do is make love and create new life. In the words of the Bible, Adam "knew Eve," and she conceives and bears Cain, saying, "I have gained a male child with the help of the Lord." What better way is there to teach us about pleasure and responsibility, behavior and consequences, than through the knowledge that the fleeting gratification of lovemaking produces a child with whom parents share a lifelong bond?

Their story depicts man and woman in their cooperative search for roles in life. In an agrarian society outside of the Garden, the roles were clearly defined: woman is to bear and nurture children, man is to provide food, tilling the soil from dawn to dusk and to protect the family. Their roles are complementary. (As Margaret Mead points out, man and woman need each other. A woman giving birth cannot be alone; she needs her man to bite off the umbilical cord.) Today, however, with the advent of birth control and the need for women to provide household income, life is far more complicated. It is exceptionally difficult for women to rear children and pursue a career simultaneously. This is a problem without a solution in sight, but it needs some sort of institutional or social readjustment because it cannot be solved by individual couples on their own. And thus the quest to define satisfying roles in life for men and women has become a great deal more complex and is always evolving.

. . .

GENERATIONS OF MALE COMMENTATORS HAVE ac-
cused Eve of being a disobedient seductress who led innocent
Adam astray, thus bringing pain and suffering—and death—to all
humankind. But a close reading of the Bible actually points in quite
a different direction.

The biblical chronicle suggests that Eve's sole motivation is
curiosity, the starting point that leads to the pursuit of knowledge
and, eventually, to wisdom. Without curiosity there is no learning,
no emotional development, no exploration of space and its elements, no improvement of the human condition, no fulfillment of
individual talents, no spiritual growth. It is Eve who forces open
the gates of Eden so that all of us may benefit from the vast, perilous realm of human potential that lies beyond the confines of the
Garden. It is her daring choice that unlocks the sexual knowledge
essential to the creation of new life.

The biblical term "to know" is an elegant summing up of the
intimate and in-depth understanding that grows over time in a sexual relationship. It means the opposite of whatever occurs in a one-
night stand. (The Bible uses words such as "come in unto you," "lie
with," for loveless couplings.) Only when a man and a woman really "know" each other over time and under many different circumstances—as companions, partners, lovers—will they risk revealing
their most private feelings and responses to each other. Only then
can the couple make love rather than have sex. The term suggests
that when a husband learns to "know" his wife, he will learn to delay his own sexual satisfaction so as to be more compatible with the
needs of his wife.

We are in this way much more advanced than animals, which are driven by instinct. (As the saying goes, the brain is the most important sexual organ.) We are the only creatures who make love facing each other, aware of our partner's expressions and feelings. Our sexual intimacies are not limited to a particular mating season or the desire to procreate. Our year-round sexual attraction to each other forges a bond that renews the connection between two human beings, strengthening the partnership so that desire, intimacy, joy, and commitment can endure into old age. The year-round sexual attraction helps maintain the structure of a monogamous society, which provides the legal and social stability that buttresses the couple, their children, and grandchildren.

The most sobering sentence in God's judgment is "Dust you are, and to dust you shall return." This is how Eve and Adam learn that life is finite. The words "from dust to dust," however, further proclaim a universal truth that is neither the tragic consequence of the first couple's disobedience nor a punishment. Our goal as humans should not be to try to escape death, but instead to embrace life and savor its challenges and gifts. The only immortality within human reach is the opportunity to be remembered by our children for our deeds and for our physical, intellectual, financial, and spiritual accomplishments. (Freud was onto something when he pointed out that love and work are the essential elements of an integrated life.)

Eve is the one who chooses knowledge over immortality. She tastes the fruit from the tree of knowledge and forgoes the fruit from the other tree, the tree of life. She manifests no interest in immortality, despite God's concern about humans' pilfering from the tree of life. The narrative implies that the trade-off of immortality for knowledge and experience is complete. When Adam and Eve become mortal, they become fully human. Death confers a sense of urgency to life; the fact of death tells us that whatever we do is important, that we must not procrastinate.

WE ARE ALL DESCENDANTS OF Eve and Adam. For the Bible, there is but one human race and we are all related. Sooner or later we find ourselves reenacting our version of the elemental story of disobedience to authority (parents, teachers) that begins with Adam but evolves through Eve, humankind's first rebel. Contrary to popular understanding, Eve is not a manipulative temptress who entraps hapless Adam; nor is she a gullible victim who succumbs to temptation. On the contrary, Eve is a risk-taker, a woman who dares to question the limitations imposed on her and her helpmate. She is driven by the need to create new life. She is the one who determines the future of humankind. She is the heroine of the story and the omniscient creator is its Author. Eve's story is the template of the stories of the biblical women that follow: women who dare to question male authority when it is unresponsive to their needs or their people's.

All along, the Divine plan relies on Eve as the partner biologically, emotionally, and mentally prepared to perpetuate the species. When she chooses to share her passion with Adam, he responds. God does not punish women for seeking "wisdom" and moving history forward. By pushing Eve and her mate out of Eden, He provides the impetus for our continuous growth and learning, as well as the circumstances that allow for human will and potential to be fulfilled through action.

Eve is a trailblazer. The biblical women who inherit the sparks of her character and follow her in the chronicles are Sarah, Rebecca, Rachel, Leah, Tamar, Naomi, Ruth, Abigail, Bathsheba, and Esther. Courageous and smart, they do not shrink from taking risks to win their husbands' love, protect their children, and ensure the survival of their kin. The women in the Bible are part of a long line of Eve's female descendants who use their powers as women to work everyday miracles in a patriarchal world.

TWO

SARAH:

THE FOUNDING MOTHER

S ARAH AND ABRAHAM LIVE A life burdened by contradictions, conflicts, and moral pressures that might well
crush the faith of ordinary mortals. God calls on this couple
to start a new life at an advanced age and promises that they will be
progenitors of a great nation. But Sarah is barren. When Abraham
is ninety-nine God tells him, "I will maintain My covenant between
Me and you, and your offspring to come, as an everlasting covenant
throughout the generations." And thus there is established the
Covenant that results in the founding of the people of Israel.

God chooses the couple to commit to the revolutionary idea
of one God in a time and place when people worship galleries of

idols. Not only is the idea of one God extraordinary, but how should one pray to a God without form, of whom no image is permitted? What does such a God expect from His believers? As the biblical scholar Nahum Sarna writes, "Israel's monotheism constituted a new creation, a revolution in religion, a sudden transformation."

"GO FORTH FROM YOUR NATIVE land and from your father's house to the land I will show you!" God tells the man then called Abram. With these words, written some four millennia ago, God propels humankind into a spiritual quest that continues to inspire hundreds of millions of people around the world, inaugurating the history of the Hebrews and weaving the first strands of the intricate fabric of spiritual innovations that define Judaism and, later, Christianity and Islam.

Abram heeds God's words. He and Sarai, as his wife was then called, leave the city of Haran, about halfway between Canaan, now Israel, and the home of Abram's ancestors, Ur of the Chaldees, now in Iraq. Trusting in God's promises, the couple set out for geographical and spiritual points unknown. He is seventy-five years old; she, sixty-five. No other major faith has had founders so aged. For us in the twenty-first century enjoying a life expectancy that extends well into the eighties, they are an exemplary couple, teaching us that we can start a new life at an advanced age, that we need not stagnate or despair as we grow old.

Most immigrants leave home and country because of poverty or persecution, but Abram and Sarai are people "very rich in cattle, silver, and gold," and the Bible makes no mention of any hardship suffered in their native land.

Though it is Abram who hears God's call, he would not have left without Sarai, his lifelong partner. Theirs is a vivid and enduring love story. They live and work as a team, both dedicated to the vision God has laid out. The biblical story implies Sarai's complete accord with Abram's decisions.

Did Sarai spend time at work or at leisure musing on her situation and concluding that there is more to life than gold and silver and a secure tent? Did she feel stirrings of wonder in her soul? Did she ponder what might be in store for her remaining years and why those additional years were granted to her? Evidently she looked for a higher purpose and a deeper meaning. How else to explain her willingness to stake their lives and possessions on a vision as revolutionary as the existence of One God, invisible and incorporeal? How else to explain her readiness to join with her husband on the long and arduous journey?

God surely observed Sarai and Abram for some time before deciding that their proven commitment to each other over many years demonstrated that they could also commit themselves to the One God. While the Bible gives no hint of God's criteria for choosing the founding patriarch, it is unlikely that He chose Abram and Sarai at random. He might have observed other couples as well but found that only Sarai and Abram lived up to His standards. As Albert Einstein put it in a very different context, "God does not play dice with the universe."

God knows that his words to Abram will not fall on barren ground. When the text introduces Abram and Sarai, the concerns of callow youth are behind them. Already elderly, they are focused on issues larger than their individual lives; in particular, they care about the beliefs and values that will transcend their life and affect the generations that will come after them. God tells Abram:

I will make of you a great nation,
And I will bless you;
I will make your name great,
And you shall be a blessing.
I will bless those who bless you
And curse him that curses you;
And all the families of the earth
Shall bless themselves by you.

Despite their being childless and Sarai's being well beyond childbearing age, the couple act on their belief in His promise by leaving home. They arrive in Canaan just as famine ravages the land that God has promised to the descendants of their yet-unborn child. To survive, Abram, Sarai, and their household continue their travels, going south to Egypt, where the Nile never fails to provide fertile silt for the fields and water for irrigation, ensuring plentiful food for its people. (During a later famine, Abram and Sarai's great grandsons likewise travel to Egypt seeking grain.) As they wind their way south through the Negev and Sinai on their donkeys, Abram and Sarai must have discussed how they and the fledgling faith for which they feel responsible can survive. Their options are few and stark as they search for a solution while sleep eludes them. Abram argues that if they enter Egypt as husband and wife, a local governor, or even Pharaoh himself, is likely to kill him, the husband, in order to seize the beautiful Sarai to add her to his harem. And if the head of the household is killed, the rest will scatter or be enslaved or murdered. Once in a harem Sarai could refuse to submit, but she would be put to death for such resistance. Abram so loves his wife that he is convinced of her being stunningly attractive to other men even at her advanced age. "I know what a beautiful woman you are", Abram tells his wife of many years.

So, if they go to Egypt as husband and wife, they both might die. Who then will carry out God's plan? At worst both they and their clan will perish and with them the new faith and nation that, in response to God's expansive blessing, they have pledged to found. At best Sarai will be forced to sacrifice her body and her honor, but Abram and their household will have a chance to survive. Before them and since their time, countless women have faced this bitter choice. The Bible later recounts, for example, the story of Esther, a young Jewish exile in Persia who centuries afterward willingly of-fers to sacrifice her life to save her people from annihilation.

In his appeal to Sarai, Abram uses the word "please," rare in the language of biblical husbands, which indicates his respect and consideration for his wife's opinions. Nonetheless, his line of argu-ment is repugnant to the modern sensibility. Abram thinks his el-derly wife is so attractive that other men will covet her, a notion that today's youth-oriented culture finds bizarre. Worse, he asks her to lie and say that they are brother and sister, knowing that this lie will mean sacrifice for her.

As night draws toward dawn, Abram, heavy-hearted and drained of ideas, awaits her response. Sarai has pondered endlessly, always forced to return to the same conclusion: she chooses the survival of the Covenant over all personal considerations. Gritting her teeth, she readies herself for the next step.

A devoted couple married for most of their long lives, they arrive at the decision independently and agree on it. Their situation is precarious. God has promised to make them a "great nation," but they and their household are facing imminent starvation and are about to enter an alien, probably hostile land where local warlords and princes are known to help themselves to the wives of shepherds passing through. As semi-nomadic foreigners they have no rights and no protectors; they are at the mercy of strongmen big and small.

Then Sarai is noticed: "Pharaoh's courtiers saw her and praised her to Pharaoh, and the woman was taken into Pharaoh's palace." The Egyptians revere Pharaoh as a living god whose every wish is a divine command. Slave women and eunuchs surely bathe Sarai, massage her, and apply fragrant oils and scents to obliterate the last traces of her wandering desert life. Shimmering robes would enhance her innate grace. Does she wonder, Will I ever see Abram again? Is my beloved husband still alive? Will he still love me after I lie with another man? Can I serve God after becoming Pharaoh's concubine?

Does Sarai sleep with Pharaoh? The Bible addresses the inescapable question only indirectly: "And because of her, it went well with Abram; he acquired sheep, oxen, asses, male and female slaves, she-asses, and camels." While this sentence strongly implies that Pharaoh compensates the "brother" for the favors of his "sister," centuries of rabbinical commentary have tended to gloss over these sisterly favors. It is not surprising that the rabbis avoided full disclosure, loath to articulate that the first matriarch of the Jewish people was forced to debase herself. Traditional commentaries piously contend that God intervened in time and Sarai was spared from Pharaoh's lust.

The salient fact is that the Bible remains silent on the denouement of the situation it has elaborately set forth. The reader's expectation is to be offered denial or confirmation of Sarai's submitting herself to Pharaoh's wish. The absence of a denial suggests—though does not prove conclusively—that she submitted. However, what seems most important from the perspective of the future of their people is that Sarai was released from the harem and reunited with Abram. The corollary to this message is that you do what you have to in order to survive and go on; what is essential is to preserve life, because without life, there is no hope.

The Bible hints that God does not allow Sarai to languish in Pharaoh's palace. God "afflicted Pharaoh and his household with mighty plagues on account of Sarai." Panic-stricken, Pharaoh summons Abram, demanding to know, "What is this you have done to me! Why did you not tell me that she was your wife? Why did you say, 'She is my sister,' so that I took her as my wife? Now, here is your wife; take her and be gone!"

Pharaoh is angry but not vengeful. He puts men in charge of Abram, and "they sent him off with his wife and all that he possessed."

When he learns the truth, Pharaoh conducts himself gallantly, contrary to the couple's fearful expectations. He may have understood that God's plagues on his house were a punishment for having abducted another man's wife into his harem. More important, God intervenes to save Sarai, the first of several miracles God enacts to protect this courageous woman so central to His vision of the future of the great people she will help found.

The episode's implications are unsettling, especially since the situation is repeated with Abimelech, King of Gerar. (In the latter case, however, God intervenes before the king had "come near her.") Some people, particularly those living in the security and plenty of a wealthy democratic society, are smug enough to charge Abram with giving his wife no option but to obey him as well as Pharaoh. But I believe the decision was considered and mutual: a deliberate, wrenching sacrifice to which they both agreed as they rode their donkeys on the long, hot, dusty trek to Egypt. (As Bertolt Brecht put it, "First food, then morals.") The key to Sarai's character is her personal strength. When in years to come a tactless concubine joins her household and threatens her marriage, Sarai's ferocity refutes any idea of meek compliance.

From Egypt, Abram and his retinue "proceeded by stages . . . to the place where his tent had been formerly" and where he had built an altar to the Lord. Back in Canaan, God lavishes Abram with increasingly grand promises of land and quantities of descendants: "I give all the land that you see to you and your offspring forever. I will make your offspring as the dust of the earth, so that if one can count the dust of the earth, then your offspring too can be counted."

But Sarai remains barren. There is no heir. While a lesser man might have made her feel guilty, Abram never reproaches Sarai for her infertility. Nor does he burden her with his growing anxiety. Instead, when he is alone out of earshot of his wife, he implores God, "What can You give me, seeing that I shall die childless?" Once again, God offers promises: "Look toward heaven and count the stars, if you are able to count them. So shall your offspring be."

Ten more years pass, and still no child.

While Abram discusses his concerns directly with God, Sarai, seething with frustration and shame, moves to break the impasse. She is humiliated both by her personal failure to bear a child, the most valued role for women of her day, and desperate that God's vision of a new nation will go unrealized. Does she run out of patience? Out of hope? Does she feel she is letting her husband and her God down?

Deliberately, resolutely, Sarai acts but, like most of us when in emotional turmoil, she does not take the time to think through the consequences of her actions. Abram never hints at taking another wife, nor does he indicate interest in other, presumably fertile women who might bear them a surrogate son—a common practice at that time. Sarai is his one and only partner, always loyal from the moment the Bible first mentions them.

"Sarai, Abram's wife, had borne him no children," the Bible says. "She had an Egyptian maidservant whose name was Hagar. And Sarai said to Abram, 'Look, God has kept me from bearing. Consort with my maid; perhaps I shall have a son through her.' And Abram heeded Sarai's request."

Sarai is legally entitled to designate her slave a surrogate mother. In her desperate yearning for a child, however, she thinks of Hagar only as a vehicle, a tool, as a means to an end. It does not occur to her that a slave woman may also have maternal yearnings. Hagar proves to be far more than a vessel for her master's progeny. Like Sarai, she has passion and—even within the strictures of slavery—ambitions of her own. Suddenly Hagar's status is elevated by the sexual attentions of the master. The equilibrium of the household gives way to jealousy and rancor.

The jealousy that tears through Sarai after encouraging her husband to bed another woman is too painful to contemplate. Privacy in the modern sense does not exist. The tents in which their household live barely muffle any sounds of lovemaking. Sarai's misery and sense of personal failure must have been intolerable as she began to worry that Hagar, once a bondwoman and now a young, fertile rival, might usurp her place in Abram's affections.

When Hagar "saw that she had conceived, her mistress was lowered in her esteem." Some commentators envision Hagar's walking by Sarai to display her protruding belly and gossiping at the well, ridiculing Sarai and burlesquing her mistress's mannerisms to sniggering maidservants. Hagar's lack of tact and bad judgment cause Sarai to find her own "plan" intolerable.

Sarai's pain erodes her reason, and she lashes out at Abram: "The wrong done me is your fault. I myself put my maid in your bosom; now that she sees that she is pregnant, I am lowered in her esteem. God decide between you and me!" She projects her misery and frustration onto Abram, even though using Hagar as a surrogate mother was entirely her own idea.

Abram, painfully sensitive to the depth of her distress, is paralyzed by the onslaught of her emotional outpouring. In an exchange that will sound familiar to many couples of our time, Abram takes the quick way out and avoids confrontation. He bolts, telling Sarai, "Your maid is in your hands. Deal with her as you think right." He leaves the women to fight it out.

Abram's terse response in the face of Sarai's anguish leads her to believe that the woman she placed in her husband's tent has taken her place in his heart. Wounded, she feels that Abram betrayed her trust. Proud Sarai, who traveled across the desert at God's command and resolutely agreed to enter Pharaoh's harem so that Abram, their household, and their faith might survive, finds she cannot bear sharing her husband with another woman. Sarai treats Hagar "harshly," and Hagar runs away into the desert.

Although Hagar oversteps the limits of her station, God remembers her. The Hebrew Bible makes the point that Hagar, though only a bondwoman, the lowliest in the social structure, is made in God's image and thus deserves attention and care. God treats Hagar with respect. Hagar is the first woman in the Bible to whom an angel of God appears. This angel finds the pregnant maid-servant "by a spring of water in the wilderness, the spring on the road to Shur, and said, 'Hagar, slave of Sarai, where have you come from and where are you going?' And she said, 'I am running away from my mistress Sarai.' And the angel of the Lord said to her, 'Go back to your mistress, and submit to her harsh treatment.' And the angel of the Lord said to her, 'I will greatly increase your offspring, / And they shall be too many to count.' The angel of the Lord said to her further, 'Behold, you are with child / And shall bear a son; / You shall call him Ishmael, / For the Lord has paid heed to your suffering. / He shall be a wild ass of a man; / His hand against everyone, / And everyone's hand against him; / He shall dwell alongside of all his kinsmen.' "

To some, this description of Ishmael sounds like a burden rather than a blessing. However, it is consistent with the genius of the biblical narrators, who present humans as complex, inconsistent beings. In this case, Hagar's son seems to be an aggressive hunter and opponent but at the same time able to live in harmony "alongside . . . his kinsmen."

God sends Hagar back to Sarai. According to the ancient tribal code of the region, Hagar is still Sarai's bondwoman and thus legally powerless to change her circumstances by running away.

Hagar gives birth to her son when Abram is eighty-six years old. In a literal sense, God's promise to Abram is fulfilled; he sires a son who will be father to a great nation, even though the mother is not his wife. According to God's instructions to Hagar, Abram names the boy Ishmael, which means "God heeds" in Hebrew.

. . .

THE PROMINENCE OF FEMALE BARRENNESS in the Hebrew Bible is puzzling. The Bible accords deep religious significance to conception and birth, miracles touched by the divine that even today still seem inexplicable by science. The milestones of conception and birth are crucial for Jews, for whom maintaining family continuity has been a central concern ever since Sarai and Abram yearned for an heir. It is precisely the concern for continuity, essential to their survival, that for Jews transforms each birth into a divine blessing.

We do not know why God subjects Sarai, exemplary in her devotion to His pronouncements, to such suffering and humiliation. Is He testing her faith in His word? Is her plight chastisement for some undisclosed sin?

Barrenness afflicts two other biblical matriarchs, Rebecca and Rachel, as well as the mothers of Samson and Samuel in later stories. From across the centuries, their voices speak to the uncounted thousands of women in our days who—despite high-tech interventions, sperm counts, donor eggs, fertility drugs—cannot become pregnant. The main difference between infertile women in ancient times and now is that today's woman can choose to define herself by roles other than motherhood, but many suffer emotional and physical pain nonetheless.

To me, the biblical emphasis on the barrenness of the matriarchs points out the importance of each individual to the survival of a minority community, by definition a people small in number. By focusing on one couple's struggle to conceive, the Bible transmutes the mundane occurrence of childbirth into a momentous event and thereby reinforces the Hebrew Bible's overarching principle that each individual is uniquely formed in the Divine image. The dignity of an individual is absolute and must be respected.

God's promises of fertility—and land—escalate.

Abram and Sarai have been in Canaan for twenty-five years—and still no child. After so many years lesser mortals might give up, concluding that parenthood is not their destiny. Yet this couple never relinquishes their dream of parenthood and founding a nation. When Abram is ninety-nine, God appears to him and reiterates, "This is My covenant with you: You shall be the father of a multitude of nations. I will make you exceedingly fertile, and make nations of you; and kings shall come forth from you. I will maintain My covenant between Me and you and your offspring to come, all the land of Canaan, as an everlasting covenant throughout the ages."

At this point God introduces a new idea—how the Covenant is to be sealed: "You shall circumcise the flesh of your foreskin and that shall be the sign of the covenant between Me and you. And throughout the generations, every male among you shall be circumcised at the age of eight days."

Astonishingly, the ritual of *brit* (Hebrew for "covenant"), or circumcision, that marked Abram's covenant with God millennia ago is still practiced today. Circumcision, performed when a Jewish male infant is eight days old, is far more than a mere surgical procedure intended to promote health and hygiene. It commits both baby and father to a sacred trust with God and the father to a sacred affirmation that the child will be reared in the faith of his fathers. This indelible mark on the flesh, the *brit milah*, lays the foundation for the infant's developing identity. It forges his sense of belonging to a continuing tradition of identity by connecting him and his faith with those who came before and those who will follow. With this Covenant God shifted the ancient Near Eastern tribal practice of circumcision from puberty to the eighth day after birth and thereby from sexual to spiritual significance.

As part of the Covenant God assigns his chosen couple new names. Abram becomes Abraham—"father of a multitude of nations"—and Sarai becomes Sarah, which means "princess" in Hebrew. Name changes mark a spiritual turning point. Sarah's grandson Jacob will have his name changed to Israel, denoting a spiritual transformation. Sarah is the only woman in the Bible whom God favors with a new name, and this honor occurs immediately after God instructs Abraham about the ritual of circumcision, which suggests her equal inclusion in the Covenant. God says, "As for your wife Sarai, you shall not call her Sarai but her name shall be Sarah. I will bless her; indeed, I will give you a son by her. I will bless her so that she shall give rise to nations; rulers of peoples shall issue from her."

Circumcision, however, marks only the male's entry into the Covenant. Why does the Bible focus on the men? Psychologically, the emphasis on father and son here is necessary because the mother is uniquely bonded to the baby by the nine months of pregnancy followed by the intense, shared experience of childbirth and then breast feeding. The infant is separated physically from its mother only after the umbilical cord is severed, and nursing starts at once.

Circumcision affords the father a central role in the child's infancy. By design, the male penis is like a heat-seeking missile, readily aroused and primed to perform its procreative function. But, as God reminds us, within reason. Every day the mark of the *brit* reminds a male that the creation of new life is a sacred duty and must

not be the casual by-product of the transitory quest for sexual pleasure. Echoing His first lesson to Adam and Eve, God's lesson to
Abraham as part of the Covenant is a lesson for every male: with fa-
therhood comes responsibility. As Abraham begins the new phase
of his life, God teaches him, "Thus shall My covenant be marked in
your flesh as an everlasting pact."

Abraham immediately fulfills his duty to God. The Bible describes how this ninety-nine-year-old first circumcises "the flesh of
his foreskin" and next circumcises his son, Ishmael, who is thirteen
years old. Despite Abraham's considerable pain, he takes his
sharpened flint and applies it until all of his household—his home-
born slaves and those bought from outsiders—are circumcised
alongside him.

ONE OF THE MOST CHARMING scenes in Genesis is a detailed domestic tableau that describes a day on which Abraham is
communing with God and enjoying the shade at the opening of his
tent by the "terebinths of Mamre." The dull ache in his groin reminds him of his circumcision and his new name; his inner calm befits the mood of a desert afternoon.

As the day grows hot, Abraham looks up and sees three
strangers. He runs from the tent to greet them. Bowing to the
ground, Abraham politely insists that they pause in their journey.
"Let a little water be brought; bathe your feet and recline under the
tree. And let me fetch a morsel of bread that you may refresh your-
selves; then go on—seeing that you have come your servant's way."

The strangers comply. Abraham hurries to the tent, eager to
serve as host to his unexpected guests. Visitors are rare in the

desert, and hospitality to travelers, a cultural obligation, provides the rest and sustenance they need to continue their journey. In the shorthand familiar to close couples of long standing, Abraham shares his excitement with Sarah and together they spring into action. Abraham nudges Sarah, "Quick, three *seahs* of choice flour! Knead and make cakes!" He dashes off to select a calf, tender and choice, and gives it to a servant boy, who hastens to prepare it. Sarah turns to her baking: under the even pressure of her practiced hands the flour quickly forms into dough that she will set to rise in the afternoon heat.

In the meantime Abraham attends to the strangers. He directs them into the shade for respite from the heat. He offers curds and milk and meat, and he waits on his guests as they eat. The couple spare no effort in this first patriarchal lesson in hospitality.

Through this simple depiction of Sarah and Abraham working in concert to make their guests comfortable, the Bible reminds us that a stranger who is dependent on us is also made in God's image and commands consideration and respect.

The visitors ask, "Where is your wife Sarah?" This is the first use of Sarah's new name, but Abraham seems unsurprised and simply replies that she is in the tent. (In fact, she is close enough to eavesdrop on the conversation, and the hem of her skirt is visible through the tent's opening.) One of the guests announces, "I will return to you next year and your wife Sarah shall have a son!"

"Abraham and Sarah were old, advanced in years," the Bible says. "Sarah had stopped having the periods of women." Upon hearing of her impending pregnancy, Sarah responds as any postmenopausal woman in her nineties would; she "laughs to herself." "Now that I am withered am I to have enjoyment—with my husband so old?" Recalling their early years, Sarah is both tickled and skeptical about the prospect of renewed passion with her elderly mate. Like many a partner in a long-standing marriage, she knows well that sex in a marriage ebbs and flows. She and Abraham have enjoyed both passion and strong sensuality, a bond that sustained them during difficult times.

When she laughs, God misunderstands, or pretends to. He says, "Why did Sarah laugh, saying, 'Shall I in truth bear a child, old as I am?' Is anything too wondrous for God? I will return to you at the same season next year and Sarah shall have a son." Like a frightened girl called on the carpet before the principal, Sarah denies her action, saying, "I did not laugh." But God insists, "You did laugh." The Bible depicts Sarah in an intriguing dialogue with God, revealing a very human side of this matriarch.

After so many years of pleadings and promises, the long-awaited child of Sarah and Abraham finally appears. Sarah's pregnancy, when it occurs at last, is clearly a result of her relationship with Abraham. It does not occur through the visitation of an angel but is conceived through the mother's sexual union with her spouse. Despite God's involvement in the timing of the child's conception, we are reminded that Abraham and Sarah are the biological parents not only of their son but also of the line that will continue their spiritual legacy.

"God took note of Sarah as God had promised and God did for Sarah as God had spoken. Sarah conceived and bore a son to Abraham in his old age, at the set time of which God had spoken. Abraham gave his newborn son whom Sarah had borne him the name of Isaac. And when Isaac was eight days old, Abraham circumcised him, as God had commanded him."

Again Sarah laughs, revealing a sense of humor, another aspect of her character hidden until now. "God has brought me laughter; everyone who hears will laugh with me," she says. And why not? Her husband is a hundred years old, she is ninety. Not only does Sarah nurse the child she despaired of ever bearing, but she also lives to rejoice a few years later with Abraham, who "held a great feast on the day that Isaac was weaned." Isaac's name, which in Hebrew derives from the word for laughter, conveys the joy of his birth.

The birth of Isaac offers Sarah yet another new beginning, launching another stage in her life and marriage. Again, at a time when many couples would be winding down, these elderly first-time parents forge ahead, their marriage reinvigorated.

Once Isaac is born, Sarah's place in the world shifts as it has for mothers before and since. Her concern for the continuity of the new faith is no longer abstract but physically real and personal. She is more than Abraham's partner and helpmate. She is Isaac's mother, revitalized by the rise of her long-thwarted maternal instinct. Fiercely, she protects her child, as his future is always first in her thoughts and dreams. Now Sarah the mother channels her spiritual goals through her bond to her child and the future she knows he must represent.

Predictably, distrust and jealousy again disturb the peace of their tent. Every time Hagar walks by, Sarah is reminded of the sleepless nights she lay alone, trying to block the image of Abraham with Hagar in another tent. She is further tormented because she knows that she herself suggested that this woman disrupt the intimacy binding her to Abraham. According to the Code of Hammurabi, the ancient Mesopotamian law, Sarah, not Abraham, owns Hagar, although Hagar, as the mother of Abraham's older son, wields some power of her own. Hagar lurks nearby, making sure that no emotional link evolves between Ishmael and his adoptive mother, Sarah.

But even as Sarah acknowledges her own turmoil, she knows no one is happy with things as they are. Abraham has strong paternal feelings for Ishmael and by extension for the boy's mother, however humble her station. Sarah's unhappiness is palpable, even if unspoken. And Hagar, who exults in her son, must always sense the resentment Sarah struggles to conceal.

Ishmael further complicates the treacherous triangle. When Sarah first suggested that her handmaid bear a son for her and Abraham, she thought she would love that son as her own. Even with the best of intentions, she now finds she cannot tolerate his presence. Ishmael's very existence reminds Sarah of the sexual relationship, and perhaps the emotional bond, between her husband and Hagar. As she and everyone in the household knows, Ishmael is Abraham's son—not hers. Now that Isaac has been born, Sarah worries obsessively about what will happen when she and Abraham die and the two boys compete for the leadership of the clan. Moreover, God has stated that Ishmael, now in his teens, will be "a wild ass of a man," virile and confident while Isaac is still young and impressionable.

Sarah can tolerate the situation no longer; Hagar and Ishmael must leave. She tells Abraham, "Cast out that slave woman and her son, for the son of that slave shall not share in the inheritance with my son Isaac." Abraham is distressed by Sarah's demand, since Ishmael is, after all, his firstborn son and he is attached to the boy. Any defense of Hagar by Abraham, however, would arouse Sarah's lingering suspicions about his feelings for the bondwoman, and the situation would become even more untenable for all of them.

Sarah is cruel to Hagar and Ishmael, but she is determined to create a strong and stable family—free of jealousy, anxiety, and suspicion. Sarah has known Ishmael all his life, was instrumental in arranging his conception. But she knows full well that as long as he remains in the family, so will his mother. She cannot, will not tolerate the "other woman" and the son who is the product of the sexual relationship with her husband.

At this point God admonishes Abraham, "Do not be distressed over the boy or your bondswoman; whatever Sarah tells you, listen to her voice, for it is through Isaac that offspring shall be continued for you." Once again God reminds Abraham that Sarah has wisdom and insight in important family matters. God advises Abraham not only to hear Sarah's words, but to listen on a deeper level for her intent and feelings.

Sarah and Hagar share prominence in this tale of passion, and God will bless them both. But the story also shows God firmly favoring monogamy by taking Sarah's side against the concubine. Hagar, in her arrogant immaturity, overestimates the power of her youth and her sexual role with Abraham. Whatever feelings flowered between them, God's unambiguous instruction to do whatever Sarah says makes it clear that the long-lasting bond between Abraham and his wife takes precedence.

Banished, Hagar and Ishmael languish in the desert. The provisions Abraham gives them—bread and a skin of water—are spent. Hagar sits at a distance from the boy. "Let me not look on as the child dies," she murmurs, and bursts into tears. (Perhaps Hagar's journey represents her unwillingness or inability to see resources— life-giving water—that are in plain view.) God recognizes the strength of Hagar's bond to her son and sends an angel who says,

"Come, lift the boy and hold him by the hand, for I will make a great nation of him." Then God opens Hagar's eyes and she sees a well. She fills the skin with water and lets the boy drink. The boy survives, becomes a hunter, and is ultimately reconciled to his half-brother Isaac, at their father's funeral.

Ishmael's banishment must have pained Abraham. Before Isaac was conceived, Abraham asked God to look after Ishmael and considered making the boy his heir. At that time Abraham said to God, "Oh that Ishmael might live by Your favor!" God replied, "Nevertheless, Sarah your wife shall bear you a son and you shall name him Isaac; and I will maintain My covenant with him as an everlasting covenant for his offspring to come."

Much is conveyed in these few lines. God teaches Abraham a lesson that must be reinforced for every father from generation to generation: women are not interchangeable vessels. God repeatedly insists that Sarah's son—not a child born to Abraham by another woman—will carry on the purposeful life his mother Sarah is committed to.

Sarah, fulfilled at last, is content with her life and the way she has lived it. She and her husband are settled, their nomadic wanderings at an end. Her only child, Isaac, has survived infancy, escaping the high infant mortality rate of the times. By sending Hagar away, and granting her freedom, Sarah ends the heartache for both women, with God's blessings. Sarah had treated her bondwoman harshly, but what kind of woman would remain calm and collected while her husband was making love with another woman in the next "room"? Soon Hagar returns to her native Egypt to find a bride for her son Ishmael. The story of both women's torment ends happily.

Sarah and Abraham resume their comfortable familiarity. As

Sarah relaxes at the opening of her tent, she keeps a keen eye on Isaac and observes the comings and goings of neighbors and the throng of cavorting children.

ABRAHAM ENVIES SARAH'S SERENITY. At night he lies awake, and like many elderly parents, he is anxious about Isaac's future. Will his son have the strength of character to adhere to the One God? Abraham, retracing the steps by which he and Sarah have tried to bind Isaac to the Covenant, is aware that he will not live to see it fulfilled. He would like to share his thoughts with Sarah but knows there are no answers to his worries. Moreover, with age Sarah and Abraham have become even more tender and sensitive to each other, and he is more determined than ever to spare her further worry and pain.

It was one thing for him and Sarah to commit themselves to serving the one God, Abraham muses. But Isaac has been given no choice. Wouldn't Isaac have an easier life worshipping along with neighboring tribes and bowing to their many gods? Abraham lives on God's promise to make his descendants a great nation, but he also recalls that God confided to him, "Know well that your off-spring shall be strangers in a land not theirs and they shall be enslaved and oppressed for four hundred years." This too is Isaac's inheritance. Will God speak to Isaac directly, as he does to Abraham and Sarah? Will God listen if Isaac questions Him the way Abraham does? If God does not enter into a direct relationship with the boy, will Isaac have the same faith in the Lord that has nurtured his parents through many years in the new land?

Now that Abraham has an heir, his anxieties take on a con-

crete form. For the first time Abraham is consumed by the fear that
his personal faith in the God who chose him will be insufficient to
sustain his own offspring through the tribulations to come. Will
Isaac succumb to the attractions of the currently prevailing idols
that he and Sarah spurned, idols that cruelly demand human sacrifice? Worse, does the God who chose him resemble those idols and
demand human sacrifice in His name? God has already told Abraham that his offspring will be enslaved and oppressed for four hundred years in a strange land. How much farther will God test the
new nation?

The story known in the Hebrew original as the Akedah,
meaning the Binding of Isaac, expresses Abraham's deepest fear.

"God put Abraham to the test. . . . He said, 'Take your son,
your favored one, Isaac, whom you love, and go to the land of Moriah, and offer him there as a burnt offering on one of the heights
that I will point out to you.' So early next morning, Abraham sad-
dled his ass and took with him two of his servants and his son Isaac.
He split the wood for the burnt offering, and he set out for the
place of which God had told him."

For the three days they travel, Abraham suffers as he tests the
limits of his belief. Sharing a faith with the majority is far easier
than being in the minority. Believing in a God who is invisible is
more difficult than believing in one who is visible. Believing in a
God who demands only blind obedience is easier than believing in
one who expects of us moral responsibility. Abraham is willing to
take on these difficulties. But now it seems his God has demanded
child sacrifice. We still see this test today being carved out all
around us. We send our sons and daughters to war for the defense
of our country and its ideals. We also see child sacrifice in unde-

clared wars in the form of suicide bombers and the boy soldiers in Africa.

With the Binding of Isaac, we see Abraham faced with a God who is demanding child sacrifice. How far is he willing to go with his belief in this God? What is the difference between his God and those of the pagan idol worshippers if his God is so cruel as to demand child sacrifice simply as a demonstration of submission to Him and not in the service of a higher ideal?

Silent and preoccupied, Abraham pushes forward, one leaden step after another. His emotions swing from his love for his son to the force of God's request. Isaac, the son he loves, on the sacrificial altar? Unthinkable. Abraham is appalled. In the course of his life and wanderings he has witnessed the grisly ritual of human sacrifice and is familiar with the sickening stench of burning human flesh. Perhaps even young Isaac has heard about such ceremonies, since offerings to the gods were customary in the region. The offerings functioned as a bribe to appease the gods, who the supplicants hoped would then provide them with bountiful crops.

Abraham walks on, faithful to the Covenant upon which he has built his life, his marriage, and his clan. Leaving behind the small group of servants, he and Isaac go forward to the designated site, carrying wood, firestone, and knife. Breaking the silence, Isaac sensibly asks, "Here are the firestone and the wood; but where is the sheep for the burnt offering?" Abraham's answer befits a devout believer unshakeable in his faith and in fact foreshadows what will happen: "God will see to the sheep for the burnt offering, my son."

"Abraham built an altar there; he laid out the wood; he bound his son Isaac; he laid him on the altar, on top of the wood. And Abraham picked up the knife to slay his son."

At that moment "an angel of the Lord called to him from heaven: 'Abraham! Abraham!' And he answered, 'Here I am.' And he said, 'Do not raise your hand against the boy or do anything to him. For now I know that you fear God, since you have not withheld your son, your favored one, from Me.'"

We, and perhaps Abraham himself, never learn what he would actually have done at the moment of truth because God is satisfied with Abraham's demonstration of his faith and ends the test. Abraham emerges from this terrifying episode haggard but reassured. His faith in the One God is confirmed; his God does not demand human sacrifice as proof of fidelity to Him. His God would never use a mother's womb—and certainly not Sarah's—as a source of human sacrifice. His God is essentially about the sanctity of human life, respecting every individual as "made in God's image."

This is God's final test of Abraham. Abraham had pleaded with God not to destroy the innocent people of Sodom and Gomorrah along with the wicked ones (he is the world's first defense attorney). He had pleaded for his promised heir multiple times before the boy was born. How could Abraham fail to ask for his only son's life? This omission suggests that Abraham is testing his relationship with God, seeing if He will refuse child sacrifice without human pleading. When God forbids it, society and culture take a huge leap forward on the path toward moral development.

In Egypt, when Abraham asks Sarah to claim she is his sister, he uses the word "please." He does not order her to obey. In the Binding of Isaac God too uses the word "please." (The text should be translated, "And God said, 'Please take your son, your favored one, Isaac, whom you love, and go to the land of Moriah, and offer him there as a burnt offering.'") God asks—He does not command Abraham to sacrifice his and Sarah's son. Abraham walks on for three days as a free moral agent who must think over what he will do.

The Binding of Isaac is a means to an end: it teaches us that this God does not demand blind obedience but instead demands constant, difficult wrestling with existential questions. It is hard to be a free moral agent who must determine what is ethical and then choose to pursue ethical behavior, whether in daily life or moments of crisis. God is satisfied with Abraham because the Patriarch demonstrated that he understands that the new faith demands a serious commitment. Believers in this God must always be alert to the consequences and implications of their actions.

The Binding of Isaac ends with God and Abraham achieving a final understanding between them. Both know the depth and commitment of Abraham's faith. Abraham now knows that his God is entirely different from the gods of his neighbors. He has reached a new plateau, a new understanding of how much he trusts his God and the nature of their relationship. That dialogue continues today in the hearts of all thoughtful believers.

SHORTLY AFTER THIS TEST, SARAH dies, at the age of one hundred twenty-seven. Rabbinical interpretation claims that Sarah dies of a broken heart after learning of the Binding of Isaac, but there is absolutely no evidence for this in the biblical narrative. The outcome of the test is reasuring, but Abraham's process of defining his relationship to God and God's demands of him is solitary, and he may never have told Sarah about the episode. He was determined to let her die in peace.

Sarah dies in Kiryat-Arba, near Hebron, twenty miles south

of Jerusalem, in the land of Canaan. Abraham "proceeded to mourn for Sarah and to bewail her." But resilient as always, he rises from his prone position next to the body of his beloved wife to attend to the details of burial in a land where he is a "sojourner." Abraham does not ask the locals for a favor or a gift, but says, "I am a resident alien among you; sell me a burial site among you that I may remove my dead for burial." After a long process of bargaining, offers, and refusals, Ephron the Hittite allows Abraham to purchase some land in Hebron, near Mamre—a field with its cave and "all the trees anywhere within the confines of that field."

Thus Abraham transforms his beloved wife's death into a memorial site for future generations that is still honored today. The matriarch was buried in the Cave of the Machpelah, which later becomes the burial place for Abraham, Isaac, Rebecca, Jacob, and Leah. Sarah remains alive in Abraham's memory for the rest of his days and in the memory of her people. Both devoted their lives to the future, taking each step in faith and believing that God's promises—of land and of abundant offspring—would come to pass. They maintained this faith despite the fact that they had no plot of land to call their own. A burial site was a start, a toehold in a promised land, a small portion of their dream made real by ownership.

The tender words of the prophet Jeremiah could well be used as a fitting summation of Sarah's life, with its triumphs and its sorrows:

I account to your favor
The devotion of your youth,
Your love as a bride—
How you followed me in the wilderness,
In a land not sown.

Just as Adam and Eve left the Garden of Eden together on their way to a brave new world, Abraham and Sarah left their comfortable old world for the land promised to them by God. Eve took risks in seeking wisdom; Sarah took risks in entering the Covenant. Many generations later their descendants will stage their exodus from slavery in Egypt to freedom in the Promised Land.

Despite the burdens imposed on them, Sarah and Abraham were dedicated to a surprisingly monogamous partnership within a polygamous society. It is impossible to think of one without the other. More than any other marriage in the Bible, that of Sarah and Abraham was a lifelong bond based on devotion to each other and a loyalty to a shared faith and vision. To the end of their life together, Sarah, at times passionate and unyielding, at times courageous and stoic, was the partner Abraham loved—and whom God sanctioned. They were inseparable.

Sarah was an outspoken woman in a male-dominated culture. She was a woman who dared, despite daunting risks. She accepted the challenge of a new faith, she spoke directly to God, and she experimented with surrogate motherhood, a risk that led to much unhappiness. Sarah is a model for women in the twenty-first century who are fortunate to live more than a third of their lives after childbearing age. Sarah is an exemplar for contemporary older women who are concerned with endowing the rest of life with a purpose and recharging old marriages with spirit and mutual interests. She defies the stereotype of the older woman stuck in a dull "old" marriage. She knew that sexual desire endures in women past the age of fertility, a trait unique to the human species. She saw to it that it continue between her and her spouse into old age. By keeping her eyes trained on the future, she forged ahead, leaving an astonishing legacy. At the same time, despite the power of her personality, the Bible shows her as vulnerable, distraught, even cruel when her marriage seemed threatened.

Not content with being ancillary to her husband, Sarah played a decisive role in the emergence of a radical spiritual idea of the One God. More than that, she saw to it that the new faith was safely and securely transmitted to the next generation. That too was her legacy. Like her descendants—especially the matriarchs who followed—she was fully engaged in the present, yet always concerned with the future. Every step of the way, Sarah was indispensable in carrying out God's grand plan. She was the tenacious, resilient, independent-minded founding mother of a people determined to keep its faith and survive.

THREE

REBECCA'S CHOICE

ISAAC GROWS UP IN THE shadow of his parents, Sarah and Abraham, two visionaries who "walked with God," talked with God, and embraced His offer of a Promised Land and His Covenant. Like other children of extraordinary parents, Isaac finds it difficult to live up to the demands of the legacy bequeathed to him. And so it is Rebecca, his wife, granddaughter of Abraham's brother Nahor, and Sarah's daughter-in-law, who shoulders the responsibility of ensuring that Sarah and Abraham's spiritual mission passes on to their descendants.

Rebecca is the outstanding leader of the second generation of the family saga. History will validate her choices, though the price she pays will be high.

. . .

AFTER BURYING SARAH, ABRAHAM AT the improbable age of one hundred thirty-seven begins to think of finding a wife for their beloved son Isaac, now close to forty years old. A gentle, peaceful man, Isaac refrains from making hard choices. "God has blessed Abraham in all things," the Bible concludes after Sarah's burial. But Abraham cannot die in peace unless he ensures that Isaac has the right wife at his side.

Abraham, anxious about Isaac's future, has reason to be worried. It is clear to him that Isaac needs a courageous, steadfast wife like his mother Sarah, to make up for the toughness he lacks. If he is to be Abraham's true heir, he must have a marriage partner with the inner resources to affirm the Covenant.

Too old and fragile to travel, Abraham calls for the senior servant of his household, in "charge of all that he owned." He asks the servant to "swear by the God of heaven and earth that you will not take a wife for my son from the daughters of the Canaanites among whom I dwell, but you will go to the land of my birth and get a wife for my son Isaac."

The servant, no stranger to the ways of the world, counters, "What if the woman does not consent to follow me to this land, shall I then take your son back to the land from which you came?" Abraham's reply is emphatic: "On no account must you take my son back there!" Abraham has never returned to his native land. He fears that his impressionable son might be persuaded to settle with his bride in her country, abandoning the Promised Land and the Covenant with God. The new faith is too fragile for a newlywed couple to withstand the influence of the seductive ways of the pagan cultures. Abraham assures his servant that God "will send His angel before you and you will get a wife for my son from there. And if the woman does not consent to follow you, you shall be then clear of this oath to me." Abraham is insistent that a bride for Isaac must not be coerced into marriage because if she does not marry voluntarily, the marriage will not become a true partnership like his and Sarah's.

It is important for Isaac to marry from among the kinship group to ensure continuity of values and identity. So Abraham sends his trusted servant on a journey of many days up north to Mesopotamia, "the old country," to find a wife for Isaac among his kinsfolk.

Taking ten camels, the servant eventually reaches the city of Sarah and Abraham's family. He lets the camels rest by a well outside the city at dusk when women come out to draw water. He prays to the God of his master Abraham, "Here I stand by the spring as the daughters of the townsmen come out to draw water; let the maiden to whom I say, 'Please, lower your jar that I may drink,' and who replies, 'Drink, and I will also water your camels'—let her be the one whom You have decreed for Your servant Isaac. Thereby shall I know that You have dealt graciously with my master." The servant's primary criteria for choosing Isaac's bride will be the character traits of generosity, kindness, and her spontaneous decisive response to a tired traveler at the well. The story suggests that when all is said and done, character is the one component we can trust in choosing our mate.

"He had scarcely finished speaking" when a woman appears with a jar on her shoulder. "The maiden was very beautiful, a virgin whom no man had known. She went down to the spring, filled her jar, and came up. The servant ran toward her and said, 'Please, let me sip a little water from your jar.' 'Drink, my lord,' she said, and she quickly lowered her jar upon her hand and let him drink. When she had let him drink his fill, she said, 'I will also draw for your camels, until they finish drinking.' Quickly emptying her jar into the trough, she ran back to the well, to draw, and she drew for all his camels."

The servant observes the maiden as she draws the water from the spring. The large earthen jar is balanced on her sturdy shoulder and braced against the palm of her upraised hand. Her conduct conveys grace and self-confidence. The Bible associates this young woman with water from the well, which sustains life in the harsh desert climate; she herself exudes the life force that the servant hopes will sustain Isaac's body and soul. He wonders if God has made his errand successful.

When the camels finish drinking, the servant gives her a gold nose-ring and two gold bands for her arms. Astonishingly, she accepts them without a moment's hesitation and with equal alacrity answers his questions about her parents' names and whether there may be room in her father's house for the servant's party.

When she says, "I am the daughter of Bethuel the son of Milcah whom she bore to Nahor," the servant knows he has found the household of Abraham's kinsfolk. And yes, there is room for the men in her father's house and plenty of feed for the camels. Without checking first with her father, Rebecca promises the servant, a stranger from another land, food and shelter for the night.

In the space of less than an hour, the Bible reveals Rebecca's character through its use of vibrant, active verbs: she "went," she "filled," she "came up," she "quickly lowered" her jar. "Quickly emptying" her jar into the trough, she "ran" back to the well to "draw" for all the camels. This depiction tells us that she is energetic, physically strong, kind and generous, and compassionate about animals. She offers to draw water for all ten camels, each of which can drink as much as twenty-one gallons in ten minutes. She knows her mind, does not hesitate, and acts confidently without seeking the counsel of her elders. Hospitality is part of Rebecca's nature, just as it was important to Isaac's parents, Abraham and Sarah. So central is this precept that the book of Genesis admonishes us not once but thirty-nine times to be kind to strangers.

Once in the house of Rebecca's father, Bethuel, Abraham's servant introduces himself and explains why he was sent to Nahor. He tells them that "the God of my master Abraham . . . led me on the right way to get the daughter of my master's brother for his son." He shrewdly reassures his hosts that Isaac is a man of property who owns sheep and cattle, silver and gold.

Rebecca participates in her own betrothal negotiations, a strikingly bold gesture in patriarchal times. Enticed by the gold jewelry the servant has given their daughter, Rebecca's family agrees to the match. But her mother and brother ask plaintively, "Let the maiden remain with us some ten days; then you may go." They know they are unlikely ever to see her again. When the servant says, "Do not delay me," they call Rebecca to ask her opinion: "Will you go with this man?" She answers, "I will." So they acquiesce and send Rebecca and her nurse off with Abraham's servant and his men.

Rebecca does not hesitate; nor does she agree with her family to delay her departure. Decisiveness and alacrity, demonstrated in the events at the well and with her family, will serve her well in the years to come.

What prompts Rebecca to follow a stranger to a strange land?

The prospect of adventure might have appealed to the spirited young woman. Or perhaps she is eager to be free of her brother, Laban, much too eager to trade her for jewels and the promise of a good match. Like all girls of her time and place, she is expected to wed, and perhaps she seizes this chance.

It is possible that throughout her childhood, Rebecca's grandfather Nahor entertained her with stories about his idealistic, passionate brother Abraham and his strong, beautiful wife Sarah. Perhaps Rebecca came to admire her great-uncle and great-aunt for their courage in striking out from Haran at God's command. Perhaps Nahor or Bethuel had also heard about Isaac, the son born to Sarah nine months after three mysterious strangers predicted she would conceive a child in her old age. Now that child, Isaac, whose name in Hebrew means "laughter," is to be Rebecca's mate. Bethuel and Laban may have been more than conventionally courteous when they tell Abraham's servant, "The matter was decreed by the Lord."

Or perhaps, blessed with a feminine combination of intuition and the self-confidence to trust her instincts, Rebecca knows that Isaac is her intended husband and yearns to play a role in the family saga.

The biblical narrative makes no mention of her feelings as she parts from her family and native land. Perhaps she finds it too painful to dwell on the farewell and refuses to think about how much she will miss them and her familiar surroundings. Perhaps she already thinks of her family as part of her past and chooses instead to focus her energy on what lies ahead. Like Sarah, Rebecca is curious and fearless, eager to "go forth" into new territory.

During the long trek to Canaan, Rebecca gives free rein to her daydreams about Isaac. Closing her eyes, she surely imagines their

first embrace. Who is this man for whom she will give up her v̶
ity and leave the family and the land she was born into? Has he hope̶
to meet a girl like her, to be his lover and the mother of his children?
Will he, like the servant Abraham sent, appreciate her modesty and
kindness, her energy and her respect for strangers? Will he be pleased
with a woman of such character who is also beautiful?

According to the customs of the day, the marriage is
arranged. Although they have never met, Isaac and Rebecca are
paired by their family because they share values, expectations, and
backgrounds. The practice of "first marriage, then love," which runs
counter to our contemporary Western assumptions about relationships, does not preclude the development of romantic feelings over
time between husband and wife. Divorce is practically unheard of in
societies where arranged marriage is the norm and in which stability
and a sense of security and trust are given priority in the institution
of marriage. Satisfaction is derived from a long-term commitment,
sharing age-old traditions and customs that are familiar to both,
strong family ties to parents, grandparents, and other relatives.
There are few of the disappointments that occur when the first
flush of passion fades and the reality of daily life faces the contemporary couple. They must weigh the exhilaration of being "in love"
against the care and attention required by a long-term emotional
and sexual relationship. In our culture, with our high rate of divorce,
we may find it helpful to consider some of the factors that make an
arranged marriage (or any long-term relationship) succeed—even
if it is strange to Western sensibilities.

Long-term relationships require commitment to the same
values, trust, compromise and flexibility, sensitivity to the emotional and sexual needs of one's partner, constant and frank com-

solving rather than vindictiveness, listening,
istic expectations rather than romantic fan-
None of these qualities sprout overnight, but
dent on a person's being in love; they can just
rranged marriage.

One evening Isaac, out for a stroll, notices camels lumbering over the horizon. As he approaches the caravan, Rebecca catches sight of him. Gracefully, she alights from the camel and asks the servant, "Who is that man walking in the field toward us?" The servant replies, "That is my master."

Modestly, Rebecca covers herself with her veil. The biblical chronicle continues in its orderly way, shifting its focus to the servant, who "told Isaac all the things that he had done." It is easy to imagine that during the long journey to Canaan the servant has recounted to Rebecca stories about Isaac, proud of his familiarity with the family. The young woman drinks it all in. Thus they are no longer total strangers when Isaac "brought her into the tent of his mother Sarah, and he took Rebecca as his wife." It is here, in the sanctuary of memories of the person he was closest to, that "Isaac loved her and thus found comfort after his mother's death."

ISAAC LOVES REBECCA. HE CAN hardly believe his good fortune, taking as his wife such a beautiful, spirited cousin half his age. They start on the highest of notes, with each finding in the other the fulfillment of all possible romantic expectations. The Bible cites an observer who spotted them through an opening in the tent wall "sporting with each other"—which might mean laughing, flirting, or perhaps much more—after all they were married.

It seems likely that with time Rebecca finds much to admire in her new husband. He is unwaveringly loyal and is not given to hasty action or intemperate words. His steady, calm disposition balances her passionate nature. The narrator could have ended here by saying that Isaac and Rebecca lived happily ever after. But this is the Bible, not a sequence of fairy tales designed to soothe the soul with comforting bromides. On the contrary, the Bible is written realistically for adults and continually alerts us to the ups and downs of marriages, the rise and fall of families, as well as the virtues and flaws of the protagonists. As with many marriages, the first days that Isaac and Rebecca spend together carry the seeds of their future trials and triumphs.

Given that Isaac has waited so long to marry and Rebecca is an eager young bride, their early lovemaking must have encompassed great passion. One may assume that to Rebecca's surprise, she soon finds herself comforting Isaac, who only now begins to heal the wound left by the loss of his mother. Living with Isaac, Rebecca must sense quickly why Abraham delayed the search for his bride until Sarah's death. As the days turn into months and the months into years, time validates Rebecca's intuition. She can see that the closeness between mother and son left no room in his affections for another woman. Isaac was the child of Sarah's old age and she was his fierce protector. Rebecca slips into Sarah's role and fills the void left by her death—a daunting task.

Gradually the newlyweds settle into a comfortable routine. Their initial exhilaration gives way to the realities created by their different temperaments. But their less-than-perfect union still proves a good-enough marriage. Isaac is easy to please and grateful to be nurtured by his capable wife. He is a peaceful man who avoids conflict and a good provider who cultivates friendly relations with neighboring tribes.

Rebecca appreciates her husband's competence in foreseeing and staving off famine. "Isaac sowed in that land and reaped a hundredfold the same year." He digs out wells that his father Abraham had dug but the Philistines had stopped up, seeing in him the threat of a rival. Local herdsmen claim the first two wells as theirs. Isaac quietly persists in digging a third, and the herdsmen finally stop quarreling. The third well remains his. He has fulfilled his family's needs without violence or revenge. He notes with satisfaction, "Now at last the Lord has granted us ample space to increase in the land."

Of all the patriarchs, only Isaac does not venture forth from the land God promised Abraham. God tells him to stay put, reiterating the oath He swore to his father: "Stay in the land which I point out to you. Reside in this land and I will be with you and bless you; I will assign all these lands to you and to your offspring, fulfilling the oath that I swore to your father Abraham. I will make your descendants as numerous as the stars of heaven." Isaac shows his constancy by physically remaining on the land while fulfilling the mandate God gives him.

Rebecca thinks often of Abraham and Sarah—their complete faith, their allegiance to God, and their commitment to the Covenant. Like Sarah, Rebecca has left behind all that is familiar. Alone with her thoughts and dreams, Rebecca finds in her faith a constant companion. She knows that it is up to her husband to ensure that the family heritage continues as the Holy One instructed. God's lessons must be transmitted to their heirs. The survival of their values, traditions, and their household, increasing in number but not yet a tribe, depends on it.

Rebecca and Isaac are a strictly monogamous couple. The sensual bond between them begins strongly, and it binds Isaac to Rebecca as his commitment to her deepens. However, for Rebecca sexual intimacy alone does not seem to compensate for what she must consciously recognize as her mounting disappointments and an increasing lack of communication between them. Whereas Sarah and Abraham are depicted as talking with each other, the Bible presents no direct dialogue between Rebecca and Isaac. When barrenness and the absence of pregnancy become painful realities, each beseeches God directly; they do not discuss these issues with each other. Later Rebecca is repeatedly shown protecting Isaac from having to confront and deal with family conflicts. She carries the burdens and worries alone.

Isaac is a wise leader in his public life, establishing a place for his family in this new land. His domestic life is a different story, however. Perhaps his fundamentally gentle nature prevents him from exerting the leadership necessary to preserve the stability of his family and lineage. Or perhaps it is the wound created by the death of his beloved mother. It is left to Rebecca to fill the vacuum created by his domestic passivity, and it is she who will be forced to make the difficult decisions concerning their family and the future of the Covenant. Decisiveness is her outstanding trait, and she assesses the challenge with the lucidity of a born leader. She doubts whether her husband is tough enough to take the necessary actions. She wonders what Isaac's charismatic father and protective, elderly mother thought of their only son's ability to lead. She resolves to help and, if required to do so, to nudge her gentle husband along to the fulfillment of his destiny.

.   .   .

LIKE SARAH, REBECCA IS UNABLE to conceive a child. Twenty years pass as Isaac and Rebecca endure the pain of their infertility. He hides his disappointment; she tries to conceal her distress. While we now know that about half of all infertility problems are traceable to the male, in the time of Genesis the women alone bear the burden of blame for their inability to reproduce. With the passing years Isaac mourns the bloom that fades from Rebecca's cheek and notes that her smile lights up her face less quickly than before. To his credit, like his father Abraham, Isaac does not forsake Rebecca for other wives who might prove fertile, as is the custom. He is strictly monogamous, and Rebecca is grateful. She appreciates her husband's positive traits rather than agonizing over his drawbacks.

It is remarkable that the male writers of the Hebrew Bible manage to convey so much of the texture and subtext of a marriage in only a few words, and particularly from Rebecca's point of view. Isaac and Rebecca have a shared concern for the future of their family and the chronic heartache of infertility, but like many couples in pain they lack the tools with which to comfort and support each other. Inside their tent they share space but not intimacy. We often hear that men and women speak different languages, that women carry the emotional burden of a marriage and find it difficult to get men to empathize with and talk about personal issues. Rebecca's story incorporates these predicaments and illuminates why she finds herself alone in implementing what God reveals to her and her alone.

Caring about each other but unable to talk freely, Isaac and Rebecca avoid bringing up painful subjects, turning instead to God.

Avoiding confrontation, they resort to circuitous means to solve their problems, increasing the distance between them by following separate emotional paths.

Isaac, like his father before him, pleads with God on behalf of his barren wife. While Abraham had to wait until the age of one hundred, God responds to Isaac's plea and Rebecca conceives when Isaac is sixty.

Rebecca's pregnancy brings new challenges. Her distended abdomen roils with movements as "the children struggle together within her." Tellingly, she does not share her pain and confusion with Isaac but instead draws on her faith and prays to God, pleading for answers and an end to her suffering. She frames her distress in existential terms, revealing her character as the most introspective and philosophical of the matriarchs. Unafraid to confront God with the fundamental existential question, she asks, "Why do I exist?" God's response gives meaning to the "struggle" within her and deepens her faith.

Two nations are in your womb,
Two separate peoples shall issue from your body;
One people shall be mightier than the other,
And the older shall serve the younger.

"When her time to give birth was at hand . . . the first one emerged red, like a hairy mantle all over; so they named him Esau. Then his brother emerged, holding onto the heel of Esau; so they named him Jacob." The name Esau derives from the Hebrew word for "hairy" or "shaggy," and Jacob, Yaakov in Hebrew, comes from the word for "heel." The Bible continues, "When the boys grew up, Esau became a skillful hunter, a man of the outdoors; but Jacob was a mild man who stayed in camp. Isaac favored Esau because he had a taste for game; but Rebecca favored Jacob."

The twins' turbulent gestation foreshadows their adult discord. Even in the womb, the boys struggle for position. They are forceful and independent long before their parents have any chance to modify their characters.

We humans are all a combination of "nature" and "nurture." For many years psychologists and child-rearing experts assumed that parents through their nurturing have the power to control the way their children's characters develop. Now, however, we recognize that genetics, peer influence, and popular culture also impact the way a child matures into adulthood. Strong genetic components in our children's personalities are present even before the day they venture into the world. These innate characteristics can be modified or strengthened by wise, patient child rearing, but the individual's unique makeup is present at birth. Acknowledging the fact that parents are not the only factor influencing their child's development will help lighten the burden of guilt so many suffer when their offspring fail or are unhappy.

Beyond the personalities they are born with, Rebecca and Isaac's twins manifest the potent, lifelong effect of birth order, which the biblical authors understood in ways remarkably compatible with modern psychology. Current thinking holds that for twins, birth order is a paramount influence on their development even when the second twin is born on the "heels" of the first, as was Jacob.

Despite their best intentions, birth order influences the way parents raise their children. This is the nurture part of child rearing, but nature figures as well. Often firstborn children are more independent, are first to try new things, enjoy special privileges, and are expected to achieve more. The children who follow must play catch-up with the firstborn, and they tend to be analytical and persistent. They often have a strong sense of fairness and may rebel against the preordained strictures of birth order as they struggle to win attention and respect.

Young Jacob and Esau play out these powerful dynamics. Isaac and Rebecca exacerbate the boys' primal rivalry by making a common but critical mistake. Each parent chooses a favorite: "Isaac favored Esau . . . but Rebecca favored Jacob." Soon after the birth of the twins, the family breaks into two factions.

Critics might call the Isaac-Rebecca union, complementary at first, ultimately dysfunctional. Either we can conclude that their relationship embodies some pathology and attach a quick label, or we can acknowledge that the marriage, though imperfect, endured. Isaac and Rebecca meet each other's basic needs: shelter, sustenance, and a modicum of companionship. Did not God say in creating Eve, "It is not good for man to be alone"? Even if we resist the temptation to burden this ancient partnership with modern expectations of intimacy and "fulfillment," these ancestors encountered the same pitfalls that have plagued couples in all of the centuries since their time.

As the boys mature, Isaac gravitates toward Esau, a boisterous, rugged, live-for-the-moment hunter who is the opposite of his cautious, placid, comfort-loving father. Isaac relishes Esau's accounts of the chase, hungering for the taste of game, and lives vicariously through adventures that his own overprotective mother, Sarah, probably forbade when he was young. Perhaps Isaac sees in Esau another Ishmael, the half brother and hunter he admired as a child but whose influence Sarah fretted over.

Rebecca, on the other hand, dotes on their second son, Jacob. In Jacob she finds a kindred spirit, so unlike the physical and restless Esau. She holds Jacob close to home, teaches him, and raises him to adhere to the ways of their Covenant. She recognizes that he has a more introspective nature than his brother does and is thus more interested in the family's legacy, its privileges, and its responsibilities.

Rebecca and Isaac succumb to a hazard common to couples who have drifted apart: they do not operate as a unified parental unit. Their relationship with their boys is a symptom of the way they relate to each other. Through their divided parenting style they unwittingly compensate for the emotional void in their marriage. Rebecca and Isaac come to depend on Jacob and Esau respectively to provide their sense of fulfillment, thereby forcing their boys to carry an unfair psychological and emotional burden. Each parent yearns for the sympathy and visible affection lacking in the marriage, and each child, eager to please—to be the "good child," is drawn into an unhealthy intimacy with one parent and a cycle of guilt with the other, always feeling he has disappointed one parent. The child plays the role of spouse to the compatible parent, and takes on the parent's struggles, investing his energies in ensuring that parent's well-being rather than concentrating on his own life and concerns.

As Jacob matures, his need for his father's approval increases. Rebecca is no longer able to meet his emotional needs as he approaches manhood. Mothers are essential to a boy's early development, but by adolescence the mother's love is viewed as unconditional, taken for granted. The son, needing independence, sees the father as more important, the parent whose approval and companionship he craves. The brothers continue jockeying for position. Jacob comes to understand the privileges and responsibilities that attach to birthright—the rights accruing to the firstborn—but free-spirited Esau considers birthright only casually, if at all. Esau is complacent, secure in his rights as the firstborn and the first in his father's heart. Jacob, on the other hand, is acutely aware that he will always be second best in his father's eyes and that the birthright he has learned to prize will always be beyond his reach.

THE FIRST RECORDED CRISIS BETWEEN the twin brothers has the cadence of an Aesopian fable.

"Once when Jacob was cooking a stew, Esau came in from the open, famished. And Esau said to Jacob, 'Give me some of that red stuff to gulp down, for I am famished.' . . . Jacob said, 'First sell me your birthright.' And Esau said, 'I am at the point of death, so of what use is my birthright to me?' But Jacob said, 'Swear to me first.' So he swore to him, and sold his birthright to Jacob. Jacob then gave Esau bread and lentil stew; he ate and drank, and he rose and went away. Thus did Esau spurn the birthright."

The vignette highlights the differences in character and temperament between the brothers. The pool of next-generation patriarchs is small indeed, and beginning with their first interactions, the biblical text goes out of its way to make clear that both the twins are flawed. Esau is impulsive and thoughtless, Jacob insecure and anxious.

Esau bursts into the scene both exhausted and invigorated by his day's hunting. The aroma of Jacob's lentil stew tantalizes him. Impetuously, he demands the "red stuff" and is so desperate to gratify his appetite right away that he trades away his birthright as casually as a modern boy unloads an outgrown bike.

As for Jacob, the episode reveals a young man who, like his mother, quickly sizes up a situation, identifies the opportunity, and acts on it. Perhaps Jacob envies Esau's physical prowess and hunting skills, but above all, he covets his twin's closeness to their father. Sheltered and schooled by Rebecca, Jacob has learned patience, sharpening his wits as a means of dealing with the brawn of other men.

Can the lentil soup passage be interpreted as a lighthearted tale of a boyish prank that goes too far? Or does the incident foreshadow a future event that will change the boys' lives forever? Or does Jacob so envy Esau's close bond with their father, Isaac, that he feels like an excluded mama's boy and gladly takes advantage of the favored firstborn? The Bible leaves it to us to discern Jacob's motivation.

The story highlights Jacob's ability to think ahead to the long term, his firm control over himself, and his resilience—all indispensable qualities in a leader. In contrast, Esau is rash. Lacking in self-discipline, he carelessly opts for immediate gratification. The stark clarity of the last sentence in the passage—"Thus did Esau spurn his birthright"—shows us that Esau is heedless of his hereditary role in the continuity of his family and the obligations of its spiritual legacy. While the stew represents the immediate present, the birthright stands for the future that is dependent on faith and fidelity.

Given his temperament, it is very possible that Esau, fleetingly wise enough to recognize his own limitations, has no wish to be burdened by a leader's responsibility to strategize and plan for the future. It is even possible that he is secretly relieved to shuck off the obligations of the firstborn.

. . .

AS THEIR BOYS REACH MANHOOD, Rebecca and Isaac are keenly aware that only one son will assume the role of patriarch. However, they deal with their concerns separately as the family saga unfolds. When trust is breached within a family, life often goes on and the ties somehow endure. So it is after Esau swaps his birthright for Jacob's bowl of stew.

The next stage in the emerging family conflict is a brief marriage announcement, inserted shortly after we read that Isaac has averted confrontation and peacefully resolved to everyone's satisfaction two potentially serious conflicts with powerful neighboring tribes. The conflicts entail wells, some dating back to the time of his father Abraham. Then, as now, water is a precious resource in the region. Then the Bible reports that Esau, now forty years old, takes as wives two local women, both Hittites. The two women, the Bible declares, "were a source of bitterness to Isaac and Rebecca."

No details are given, but it is easy to surmise why Esau's choice upsets both his parents. Abraham has already made it clear that his progeny are to marry from within their own tribe in Mesopotamia, and he stipulated in particular that Isaac not marry a Hittite woman from Canaan. To Isaac, and especially Rebecca, Esau's marriage to two idol-worshiping Hittites clearly signals a lack of commitment to, if not outright rejection of, God and the Covenant with Abraham and Sarah. A foreign wife is unlikely to support his following the ways of his ancestors and at worst may well lead him astray. If Esau becomes Isaac's successor and is not staunch in his faith, the entire household, and the nation, is in danger of disintegration.

What follows the terse marriage announcement is one of the

Bible's most artfully—and theatrically—crafted scenes. The text draws us into the tense moment when the legacy of Abraham and Sarah teeters precariously between two rivals. Rebecca confronts a heart-wrenching choice.

Isaac has become blind and infirm. He calls his firstborn, Esau, and says to him, "I am old now and I do not know how soon I may die. Take your gear, your quiver and bow, and go out into the open and hunt me some game. Then prepare a dish for me such as I like, and bring it to me to eat so that I may give you my innermost blessing before I die."

Rebecca eavesdrops on her husband and firstborn son. Not one to leave anything to chance, she waits for her opportunity to act. After Esau leaves to hunt game Rebecca tells Jacob, "I overheard your father speaking to your brother Esau, saying, 'Bring me some game and prepare a dish for me to eat that I may bless you with the Almighty's approval before I die.' Now, my son, listen carefully as I instruct you. Go to the flock and fetch me two choice kids and I will make of them a dish for your father such as he likes. Then take it to your father to eat in order that he may bless you before he dies."

Uneasily, Jacob protests, "But my brother Esau is a hairy man and I am smooth-skinned. If my father touches me I shall appear to him as a trickster and bring upon myself a curse, not a blessing." But Rebecca is firm, her mind made up. She says to Jacob, "Your curse, my son, be upon me! Just do as I say and go fetch them [the goats] for me."

As Rebecca talks the reluctant Jacob into wresting Isaac's blessing intended for Esau for himself she parlays Isaac's instructions to Esau to her own purposes. Here is the opportunity to undo the consequences of birth order and ensure the succession of the son who is more apt to live up to his heritage. Throughout her life Rebecca, like other women of her times, has been governed by traditional social strictures and patriarchal authority. As Jacob's doting mother, perhaps she believes she will be assured influence as she devotes her talents to help Jacob run the affairs of the household, found the new nation, and steer it into the future.

Jacob, eager for the blessing that will change his fortunes and vault him over his brother, nonetheless balks at his mother's feverish instructions, reluctant to deceive one parent or disobey the other. Moreover, Jacob is uncertain that the chance at the blessing is worth any curse he might incur if Isaac notices the deception.

Rebecca is not to be deterred: her beloved Jacob is too close to the leadership position that God ordained for him. As Jacob squirms and protests, she repeats, and we can almost hear her, "Your curse, my son, be upon me! Just do as I say." With these words, Rebecca assures her son that she will bear the responsibility for the consequences of deceiving his father. Jacob has neither the heart to disappoint his mother nor the strength to resist her wishes.

Jacob fetches the kids for Rebecca, who hastens to prepare the dish his father prefers. Rebecca takes Esau's hunting clothes and talks Jacob into putting them on. She covers Jacob's smooth hands and the hairless part of his neck with the skins of the kids. Then she gives Jacob the goat stew and the bread she has prepared.

"He went to his father and said, 'Father.' And he said, 'Yes, which of my sons are you?' Jacob said to his father, 'I am Esau, your firstborn; I have done as you told me. Pray sit up and eat of my game, that you may give me your innermost blessing.' Isaac said to his son, 'How did you succeed so quickly, my son?' And he said, 'Because the Lord your God granted me good fortune.'"

Isaac, suspicious, asks Jacob to come closer so that he can feel him to determine whether he is really Esau. "So Jacob drew close to his father Isaac, who felt him and wondered. 'The voice is the voice of Jacob, yet the hands are the hands of Esau.' He did not recognize him, because his hands were hairy like those of his brother Esau."

For the last time Isaac asks, " 'Are you really my son Esau?' And when he said, 'I am,' he said, 'Serve me and let me eat of my son's game that I may give you my innermost blessing.' So he served him and he ate and he brought him wine and he drank. Then his father Isaac said to him, 'Come close and kiss me, my son.' And he went up and kissed him. And he smelled his clothes and he blessed him, saying, 'Ah, the smell of my son is like the smell of the fields that the One God has blessed.' "

Not once but three times Isaac questions the identity of the son before him, the son who says he is Esau. Isaac's eyes are too dim to see, but his other senses are sharp. He draws on each of them in turn, to confirm the son's identity. As suspense builds, Isaac marvels that while he hears the voice of Jacob, he feels, as he touches his son, the hairy hands of Esau. Again he asks, "Are you really my son Esau?" Then he tastes the food and drinks the wine. Finally, Isaac pulls Jacob close to him and smells his clothes. After all this questioning, he blesses him.

Isaac questions Jacob's identity three times, and after Jacob lies three times, Isaac's words are accepting. But he refrains from saying "Esau" and instead says "my son" three times: "let me eat of my son's game," "kiss me, my son," and "the smell of my son is like the smell of the fields." The person he ends up blessing is the one playing the role of eldest son. Isaac's choice of words seems to acknowledge his complicity in the choice of heir.

Through this sequence, Isaac appears to be increasingly suspicious that it is in fact Jacob before him. Yet Isaac goes along with the deception, I believe, knowing all along that Esau lacks the leadership to carry out Abraham's legacy.

The blessing Isaac gives Jacob has beauty and assures him of future leadership and power over his enemies, abundance of food and wine:

> *May God give you*
> *Of the dew of heaven and the fat of the earth,*
> *Abundance of new grain and wine.*
> *Let peoples serve you,*
> *And nations bow to you.*
> *Be master over your brothers.*
> *And let your mother's sons bow to you.*
> *Cursed be they who curse you,*
> *Blessed they who bless you.*

"No sooner had Jacob left the presence of his father Isaac—after Isaac had finished blessing Jacob—than his brother Esau came back from his hunt. He too prepared a dish and brought it to his father. And he said to his father, 'Let my father sit up and eat of his son's game, so that you may give me your innermost blessing.' His father Isaac said to him, 'Who are you?' And he said, 'I am your son, Esau, your first-born!'

"Isaac was seized with very violent trembling. 'Who was it then,' he demanded, 'that hunted game and brought it to me? Moreover, I ate of it before you came and I blessed him; now he must remain blessed!' When Esau heard his father's words, he burst into wild and bitter sobbing and said to his father, 'Bless me too, Father!' But he answered, 'Your brother came with guile and took away your blessing.' [Esau] said, 'Was he, then, named Jacob that he might supplant me these two times? First he took away my birthright and now he has taken away my blessing!' And he added, 'Have you not reserved a blessing for me?' Isaac answered, saying to Esau, 'But I have made him master over you; I have given him all his brothers for servants and sustained him with grain and wine. What, then, can I still do for you, my son?' And Esau said to his father, 'Have you but one blessing, Father? Bless me too, Father!' And Esau wept aloud."

Hearing his son's cries, Isaac's heart must have been broken. However, there was ample paternal love left for Esau. "And his father Isaac answered, saying to him, 'See, your abode shall enjoy the fat of the earth and the dew of heaven above. Yet by your sword you shall live, and you shall serve your brother; but when you grow restive, you shall break his yoke from your neck.'"

With Rebecca's behind-the-scenes stage managing, Isaac blesses Jacob, the son who will inherit Abraham's legacy. Rebecca takes on the role of Sarah, who persuaded Abraham to banish his firstborn son, Ishmael, born to Sarah's bondwoman Hagar, so that Isaac, her only child, could be unchallenged in the succession to Abraham. But choosing her husband's successor was more difficult for Rebecca than for Sarah because the child passed over was also her own son, not her rival's.

When Esau comes to claim the blessing, Isaac, agitated, is seized with a "very violent trembling" as he at last assumes his role as the patriarch, the destiny set out for him at birth. As he begins to function as the patriarchal leader, he both transfers that role to Jacob and denies Esau the innermost blessing that the older son blithely assumed he would inherit all along.

Today lawyers would argue that Isaac's blessing was invalid due to fraudulence, because Rebecca and Jacob deliberately deceived Isaac. Four thousand years ago, however, the practice of nomadic tribes held that an action invoking God's name was irrevocable. As Isaac speaks, he calls on God to carry out the blessing. There is no chance for second thoughts, no room for revision, no turning back.

The ancient transaction is fortified by yet another ceremony: Isaac touches Jacob. Although the text repeatedly states that Isaac believes he is blessing Esau, Jacob's physical presence at the blessing ceremony carries greater power than Isaac's articulated intent and overrides any verbal protest Esau might raise. As Isaac touches Jacob, probably resting his rounded palm on Jacob's bowed head, Jacob absorbs the blessing physically. In accordance with the laws of the time and the place, such a blessing is valid no doubt because agreements were oral, rather than written.

Throughout their marriage Rebecca protects Isaac from the burden of difficult family decisions and emotional turmoil. He excels in managing his crops and his flocks; he deals peaceably and productively with difficult neighbors. He makes sure his family is prosperous and safe. Isaac fulfills the role of a transitional figure, the stabilizer who sinks roots in the land and forges the link between the first generation and the third generation of the patriarchs. But within the tent Rebecca takes over. The women of the Bible are essential partners with their men in handing down God's Covenant from one generation to another. Did not God highlight the mother's crucial role when He said to Abraham, "Do as Sarah says"? They are, as in the story of Eve and Adam, a structural element, a "rib," that, if removed, leads the family to fall apart.

Was Isaac pathetically deceived or tacitly complicit? I believe that in handing down the all-important blessing to his heir, Isaac is Rebecca's silent partner. Engaging in the charade of mistaking Jacob for Esau is Isaac's way of sparing Esau's feelings, or perhaps his way of not having to actively acknowledge that Jacob is in fact better suited to be a leader of men and nations than his favorite, Esau.

ESAU, FURIOUS AT BEING DISINHERITED, vows to "kill my brother Jacob." When Rebecca learns of this, once again she quickly conceives a plan and tells Jacob, "Flee at once to Haran, to my brother Laban. Stay with him a while, until your brother's fury subsides—until your brother's anger against you subsides—and he forgets what you have done to him. Then I will fetch you from there."

As she speaks, her words renew the memories of the girlhood home she so readily abandoned, and of the mother's love she needs now as never before.

Next Rebecca approaches her husband. Just as she shielded him from openly facing the decision of choosing an heir, she once again protects him from the knowledge that Esau plans to kill his brother by not revealing the true reason for Jacob's imminent departure. Instead, she begs Isaac to send Jacob to Paddan-aram, to the house of Bethuel, her father, to find a wife there among the daughters of Laban, her brother. Jacob must not repeat Esau's error, diluting and scattering their line through intermarriage with peoples who do not share their fledgling faith. Rebecca cries out to Isaac, "I am disgusted with my life because of the Hittite women. If Jacob marries Hittite women like these, from among the native women, what good will life be to me?" Rebecca is emotionally distraught. She has just overturned the traditional rule of primogeniture; one son has threatened to kill another; she fears her elder son's bond to the Covenant will be weakened by his marriage to local Hittite women; and she worries that the new heir will similarly choose a wife without ties to their family or faith.

Isaac immediately sends for Jacob and says to him, "You shall not take a wife from among the Canaanite women. Up, go to Paddan-aram, to the house of Bethuel, your mother's father, and take a wife there from among the daughters of Laban, your mother's brother. May El Shaddai [another term for God] bless you, make you fertile and numerous, so that you become an assembly of peoples. May He grant the blessing of Abraham to you and your offspring, that you may possess the land where you are sojourning which God gave to Abraham." In the end Isaac echoes God's words to Abraham. As Isaac discharges his responsibilities, living up to his role as his father's heir, the last word he utters is "Abraham" the circle is now complete, the chain unbroken.

As Rebecca's story draws to a close, she doggedly protects the continuity of the family's legacy despite the terrible risks. If Esau carries out his threat and kills Jacob, not only will the tragedy be unbearable, but the spiritual journey initiated by Abraham's faith will end prematurely.

With sinking heart, Rebecca creates an optimistic fiction, telling Jacob their separation is temporary. She fears she will never see her younger son again, just as she never saw her own family after she left to marry Isaac. But separation from her son is less intolerable than the prospect of his dying by his brother's hand. In fact, she never stopped loving Esau, even while disapproving of his lifestyle and his decisions. Her agony is revealed in her last plea as she attempts to speed Jacob's departure: "Let me not lose you both in one day!"

Up to this point, Esau has focused his wrath on Jacob, but Rebecca might very well fear that he will soon discover her role in the deception and will harden his heart toward her. Her husband is approaching senility, her younger son has had to flee and Esau has been absorbed into the alien Hittite culture. Rebecca's loneliness is complete.

REBECCA IS THE ONLY WOMAN in the Bible we follow from maidenhood through the span of her marriage. Her story demonstrates the human capacity to make free and moral choices. Free will is what is meant by being made in the image of God. Choice is inherently accompanied by anxiety and accountability. We are accountable for the consequences of our decisions and we must bear the pain, even when we have made the right choice.

Some find Rebecca deceitful. What I see is that her talent and drive expand to fill the vacuum created by her husband's lack of leadership within the confines of his family. She has no institutional power in the social structure of her day, and so she is forced to be crafty and cunning instead of acting openly. Once she accepts responsibility for the next generation of her family, she has no tools to wield, so she must work around her husband. Over the years she and Isaac have seldom discussed personal matters, and he has made his preference for Esau clear. Now he is old, blind, and failing, and more interested in the here and now (for example, the game Esau brings back from the hunt). Rebecca, on the other hand, stays focused on the future. Lacking someone with whom to discuss the matter, she subverts her husband's authority and secures the blessing for Jacob because she understands that God's covenant is at stake. She braces for the consequences.

Our hardest decisions fall in the gray areas of life. When issues are black and white, the decisions are simpler. Rebecca is conscious that her decision is freighted with historical consequences. But Jacob, with his self-discipline and introspective nature, is better qualified to be the next standard-bearer than the impulsive, shortsighted Esau. Rebecca must deal with the reality before her, and her painful choice ensures the survival of the tribe.

Even if she had been in a position to appoint the heir openly, heartache was inevitable because in this family the biological heir—the firstborn—was not the son with the most leadership potential. This situation occurs frequently in family businesses and royal houses when the next generation is to take over. On the other hand, Rebecca's having to work through subterfuge exacted a heavy price from her family: Isaac was implicated in deceit, Jacob felt guilty, Esau was furious. An open discussion would have been hurtful to Esau, but the reasons could have been explained and the final decision would not have ambushed him. However, Rebecca did the best she could within the context of her marriage and the times she lived in.

Rebecca's story shows us that conflicts are built into the family structure. No matter how much we love each child, there is always more to give, and each child yearns for more. Throughout the generations of Sarah and Abraham's family, we see that family harmony is not offered to us on a silver platter and that sibling relationships are fraught with tension, especially when entwined with issues of power and inheritance.

In the stories of Genesis we see the early seeds of democracy. Tradition stipulates that the firstborn son inherits power and property, but Genesis shows that these legacies must be earned by merit instead.

Could Rebecca have chosen other ways by which to carry out

God's plan, and did God always approve what she did? Could she have arranged the succession so the loser would not have been reduced to sobs and thoughts of vengeful murder? How did she weigh the damage to family harmony against the higher goal of ensuring future leadership? Could she have kept Esau and his descendants within the tribe of Abraham? Or did Esau's values—and Ishmael's before him—deviate from the faith of Sarah and Abraham so widely that a parting of the way was inevitable? Was it her responsibility to make sure that God's prophecy was enacted, His promise that "the older shall serve the younger"?

All the Bible tells us is what choice she made, not how she arrived at it. The great first-century scholar Rabbi Akiva, who lived through the destruction of the Second Temple, summed up the contradictory paradoxes of life when he said, "All is foreseen, but freedom of choice is given." When Rebecca is with child, God tells her what will be, but He does not tell her how it will come about: she is responsible for the individual choices she makes every day that lead to the outcome foreseen by God. It is precisely the tension between human freedom and God's will that characterizes so much of human "wrestling" with ethics in the biblical narrative. But free choice also means that we cannot scapegoat God for what we choose to do.

Rebecca works alone. When Sarah, a mature woman, arrives in the Promised Land, she is a partner in a long-standing relationship marked by love and devotion. The couple worked in tandem, arriving at momentous decisions together, and when Sarah felt a rival was taking her place, she spoke up in no uncertain terms.

Unlike her mother-in-law, the young Rebecca arrives alone in a strange land to marry into the second generation of remarkable family founders. Isaac loves her, and she is committed to their arranged marriage, to mutual loyalty and solidarity.

Unlike Sarah and Abraham, Rebecca and Isaac function as two separate entities held together by their shared belief in their Covenant with God and in the responsibilities and privileges that go along with it. There is mutual loyalty and fidelity but none of the passion that their elders felt for each other.

In the age of therapy one hears Rebecca and Isaac's marriage cavalierly dismissed as dysfunctional. There is no such thing as a risk-free life. The humanity of their story comes across the centuries in the realistic description of a marriage between two imperfect human beings dealing with moral dilemmas when the choices are in the gray areas of life and consequences exert a heavy price. The marital dynamics, the couple's strengths and weaknesses make it possible for us to identify with them thousands of years later.

Were their issues that different from ours? Not really. Theirs is an archetypical story depicted with bold, broad brushstrokes. Generation after generation we draw from, reinterpret, and apply its moral, spiritual, and psychological insights to our personal lives today.

Rebecca and Isaac's monogamous marriage endured and in today's parlance would be described as "good enough." Their primary responsibility was to ensure that the founder's vision was safely handed down to the third generation. Thanks to Rebecca, they succeeded.

FOUR

Rachel and Leah,
and Their Husband, Jacob

TWO SISTERS, LEAH AND RACHEL, are both mar-
ried to Jacob, the most troubled of the patriarchs and the
third standard-bearer of the family founded by Abraham
and Sarah, his grandparents. The story of Jacob and his wives
throbs with passion, envy, misery, and pride. It is in this generation
that the family increases in number and God's promises projecting
a people "exceedingly numerous" no longer seem implausible.

AFTER SUPPLANTING HIS FIRSTBORN TWIN, Esau, as
Isaac's heir, Jacob is racked by multiple anxieties. At Rebecca's

frantic urging he has fled Beersheba, his birthplace, to seek refuge with her kinfolk in Haran, his mother's birthplace in Mesopotamia. For the first time in his life Jacob is on his own, no longer protected and advised by his mother, who has always favored the quiet, introspective Jacob over the impulsive, rough-hewn Esau. As his camel carries him farther and farther from his home he rues the new course of his once-comfortable life. Well aware that his father's blessing was not earned honestly, Jacob will stay away from home for many years. As he travels, sounds from the far reaches of the plain spark Jacob's fear that Esau, enraged by the loss of his rights as firstborn, is in hot pursuit, eager for revenge.

One night "he came upon a certain place and stopped there for the night, for the sun had set. Taking one of the stones of the place, he put it under his head and lay down in that place. He had a dream; a ladder was set on the ground and its top reached to the sky and angels of God were going up and down on it. And the One God was standing beside him and said, 'I am the God of your father Abraham and the God of Isaac. The ground on which you are lying I will give to you and to your offspring. Your descendants shall be as the dust of the earth; you shall spread out to the west and to the east, to the north and to the south. All the families of the earth shall bless themselves by you and your descendants. Remember, I am with you: I will protect you wherever you go and will bring you back to this land. I will not leave you until I have done what I have promised you.'"

The ladder is unanchored yet steady and its top floats in the heavens. This rich image suggests an escape route from the psychological crossroad Jacob finds himself in, a period of transition from his difficult past to a hopeful future. It is phallic, as befits the dream of a young man in search of a wife. It also signals spiritual ascent:

Jacob's prayers rise to heaven and in return reassurance from God flows down to him.

Stunned, "Jacob awoke from his sleep . . . then made a vow, saying, 'If God remains with me, if He protects me on this journey that I am making, and gives me bread to eat and clothing to wear, and if I return safe to my father's house—the Lord shall be my God. . . . and of all that You give me, I will set aside a tithe for you.' " At this point Jacob's faith is uncertain. He has never had to test his own beliefs or abilities in the world outside the familial tents.

As Jacob matures he will move past his unseemly, self-serving bargaining with God, but at the beginning of his passage into the unknown he is still an insecure, self-absorbed young man who, in addition to being young and untested, carries the burden of the past in his soul. Like many young people, he has little past experience to rely on and his uncertainty about his own place in the world drives him to seek signals from others that he is indeed worthy. Furthermore, his journey toward maturity necessitates his separation from his parents and family. Jacob questions the mutual commitment between God and his family by setting conditions and making self-serving bargains with God. He indicates that he will believe and trust only if his life is secured and he is eventually able to return home.

The lonely fugitive hears God's promise—"I am with you: I will protect you wherever you go"—words that evoke God's promise to his grandfather, Abraham: "Fear not . . . I am a shield to you." The words of parents to their children have a powerful effect; children take these words to heart so that the messages become integral to who they are. Jacob absorbs God's promise of divine protection and experiences His voice as if it were his very own. Hundreds of years later the same feelings and the same trust in

God's protection are expressed in David's Psalm 23: "The Lord is my shepherd; I shall not want . . . though I walk through the valley of death I will fear no evil, for Thou art with me." As Jacob continues on his journey he begins to build the inner resources that will sustain him through a life of family tragedies and spiritual triumphs.

Jacob's fear of harm abates with each mile that separates him from Esau, but he is vulnerable, exhausted, and hungry for human warmth and kindness. As he approaches Haran he notices a well, just as Abraham's servant did when he encountered the young Rebecca and knew instantly that she was the bride destined for Jacob's father, Isaac. The human body is about sixty percent water, and water is necessary for the survival of humans, animals, and plants. Water is life-giving and because so much of the Middle East is dry, people from that region are particularly aware of its role. The well also symbolizes the womb that will give life to Jacob's numerous future offspring. Jacob sees that this well is in the open, surrounded by three flocks of sheep waiting for their time to drink after someone rolls aside the large stone covering the mouth of the well. He knows he has reached his destination when he hears the men standing by the well talk about Laban, his mother Rebecca's brother, and mention that Laban's daughter Rachel should be on her way to the well.

"While he was still speaking with them Rachel came with her father's flock; for she was a shepherdess. And when Jacob saw Rachel, the daughter of his uncle Laban, and the flock of his uncle Laban, Jacob went up and rolled the stone off the mouth of the well and watered the flock of his uncle Laban. Then Jacob kissed Rachel and broke into tears." Jacob's pent-up anxieties and longings come to a head and with that first passionate kiss, the die is cast.

When Jacob sets eyes on Rachel his yearnings find their home.

Smitten by her beauty, he shows off his manly strength by hefting the stone cover from the well. This is the new, physically active, virile Jacob, no longer tied to his mother's apron strings and unafraid of being tested. There is a subtle symbolism here as the lifting of the stone from the well foreshadows Rachel's loss of virginity and her impending change of status from virgin to wife. But the weight of the stone also signals the obstacles that will stand in the way of Jacob's consummating his love for Rachel. The impulsive kiss and the tears that follow seal Jacob's fate. He will always be in love with Rachel. Through all that follows—wives, children, concubines, and soul-wrenching crises of faith—Rachel remains the love of Jacob's life, as Rebecca was to his father and Sarah to his grandfather.

Stunned by Jacob's bold greeting and thrilled by the arrival of an unexpected cousin from a faraway land, Rachel runs to report to her father. Jacob proceeds to tell Laban all that has happened to him and Laban says, "You are truly my bone and flesh." Laban's polite, seemingly warm greeting masks his true nature which is scheming and greedy. But Jacob alone, a stranger in a strange land, is in no position to judge his "new" uncle.

"Now Laban had two daughters. The name of the older one was Leah and the name of the younger was Rachel," the Bible notes. "Leah had weak eyes; Rachel was shapely and beautiful." Jacob loves Rachel. Being entirely without means, he can offer only his labor in exchange for her and extravagantly offers to serve Laban seven years. Laban does not refuse this bargain and tells Jacob, "Better that I give her to you than that I should give her to an outsider. Stay with me."

Jacob shows the stuff he is made of: patience, passion, and hard work. "So Jacob served seven years for Rachel and they

seemed to him but a few days because of his love for her." With
these spare words the Bible conveys the intensity of Jacob's attachment to Laban's younger daughter. (Many commentators have sur-
mised that what the Bible means by "years" is probably different
from the 365 days of today's years.) When the seven years come to
an end, Jacob approaches Laban in businesslike fashion: "Give me
my wife, for my time is fulfilled, that I may go in unto her." As was
the case when Jacob's father, Isaac, failed to name Esau in dispens-
ing his blessing to Jacob, Jacob's own lack of specificity eases the
way for deception. If Jacob had said "Give me Rachel" instead of
"my wife," Laban might have had more difficulty substituting Leah
for Rachel under the wedding veil.

Laban, a wealthy man, prepares an extravagant wedding
feast. The wedding, the fulfillment of Jacob's anticipations, is perhaps the happiest time in his short life, but it ends in a startling deception and a familial betrayal. As evening falls Laban, concealing
Leah's face with a thick black veil, brings her to Jacob's tent. In the
morning light Jacob discovers the trick, rushes to Laban, and cries
out, enraged, humiliated and helpless; "Why did you deceive me?"

The Bible does not say whether it occurs to Jacob that this
ruse parallels his own deception of his father. In misleading Isaac,
Jacob relied on the dimness of his father's eyes just as the cunning
Laban used the darkness of the night to substitute the older daughter for the younger. Is it possible that Jacob was so intoxicated with
wine and passion that he was blind to the fact that it was Leah in his
arms and not his beloved Rachel? Laban asks Jacob to complete the
"bridal week" to spare Leah from disgrace and tells him that he may
then marry Rachel. And the lovesick Jacob agrees to serve Laban
for seven more years after marrying Rachel.

We can only guess how the sisters must have suffered. Does

Jacob whisper Rachel's name while embracing Leah on her wedding night? Is Leah's heart breaking as she grieves for the love she does not have? Should Leah have resisted her father's machinations, or was she his silent partner in the deception—as her father-in-law, Isaac, may have been with his wife, Rebecca? Or was Rachel also a silent partner with her father and sister? Was it her way of "taking care" of her plain older sister, secure in the knowledge that she would not lose Jacob's desire for her?

Was Rachel who waited for seven years only to watch her sister and Jacob enter the tent truly distraught when Leah usurped her place in the marriage bed? Did Rachel lie awake through seven endless nights, pressing her eyes shut against the vision of Jacob touching Leah, bestowing caresses meant for her? Or did Rachel perhaps not care intensely for Jacob but resented being upstaged by her sister? Was Rachel powerless to disobey her father's decisions? Jacob's wedding night is fraught with mystery. The questions are the same, but the answers vary.

In this story the Bible demonstrates a preference for monogamy by detailing the miseries of polygamy. Polygamy is shown to encourage rivalry among multiple wives to gain the single husband's sexual and emotional attention, to have the most children, to receive the most kudos, and to gain the most favor for their children. Further, polygamy is shown to dilute the intensity of feeling that is possible only between one man and one woman.

Modern men may fantasize about a plethora of available women, but the Bible depicts polygamous men as forced to deal with the politics and rivalry among their wives and their children, a rivalry that often extends into the next generations. It offers the sobering suggestion that the husbands (such as Jacob with Rachel, Abraham with Sarah, and Elkanah with Hannah) endured unhappy domestic lives because they had to deal with the misery and suffering of many women, but above all of the woman they loved most.

Rachel and Leah eventually learn to accommodate to a situation they have no power to change, but their accommodation does not imply that they are contented women. Their father is the head of the family and his word is law. Because of his greedy conniving and eagerness to exploit free foreign labor the two sisters and Jacob are locked into a triangle in which none can be fully satisfied. Reluctantly, Jacob, Leah, and Rachel are forced to learn to accommodate jealousy, confusion, and hurt.

By the time Rachel and Jacob are wed Rachel seems to function not so much as a wife but as a mistress—the "other woman" recognized the world over. The biblical account is spare and factual: "And Jacob cohabited with Rachel also; indeed, he loved Rachel more than Leah." Rachel is available to Jacob emotionally and sexually whenever he wishes. She is childless for a long time and the day-to-day tasks of child rearing do not intrude or dilute the intimacy of their relationship. She must defer to his first wife and the mother of his children and their demands on his time. She cannot allow herself to express feelings of jealousy or anger about the first wife or the wife's children, nor give voice to her yearnings for a home and children of her own. Like a mistress she may well be Jacob's favorite as long as she does not threaten the basic stability and rules of their relationship. As we shall see, the role of the "other woman" is not what Rachel wishes: she yearns for a maternal role in Jacob's family, like that of her fertile sister Leah.

. . .

"AND GOD SAW THAT LEAH was unloved and opened her womb; but Rachel was barren. Leah conceived and bore a son, and named him Reuben; for she declared, 'It means: "The One God has seen my affliction"; it also means: "Now my husband will love me."' She conceived again and bore a son and declared, 'This is because the One God heard that I was unloved and has given me this one also; so she named him Simeon. Again she conceived and bore a son and declared, 'This time my husband will become attached to me, for I have borne him three sons.' Therefore he was named Levi. She conceived again and bore a son, and declared, 'This time I will praise the One God.' Therefore she named him Judah. Then she stopped bearing."

Leah loves Jacob wholeheartedly. She might have fallen in love with him during their week in their marriage tent when she forged a lifelong sexual bond with a man who spent the same week fantasizing about her sister. However, it is equally plausible that Leah had set her heart on Jacob earlier, during the seven years he labored for Rachel. Leah longs to be the center of Jacob's life, to be uniquely accepted, even treasured, in a way that is possible only in a monogamous, sexually exclusive relationship. Leah's tragedy is that sex cements her attachment to Jacob, her only lover, but Jacob's primary sexual and emotional attachment is to someone else. Their feelings for each other are out of balance from the very start, and Jacob's emotional withdrawal from Leah might have been exacerbated by the fact that she was forced on him. A throng of children surrounds Leah, but they cannot compensate for Jacob's emotional distance from her. As the years go by her heartbreak only deepens.

The meanings of the names Leah gives her first three sons reflect her frustration as each successive birth fails to win Jacob's love. At first she relies on God to make Jacob love her, then takes comfort in the filial love from her sons and moves on to believe that Jacob will love her because they share three sons together. As the years come and go her body is just finished bearing one son when Jacob visits her for a night and launches another pregnancy. Unloved, Leah learns through the years to draw strength from her role as mother.

The turning point comes with the birth of Judah, her fourth son. She begins to grow into her role as matriarch, secure in her identity and status within the family. With Judah she undergoes a transformation. After three sons she stops defining her worth by her husband's lack of love and, instead, thanks God for the fourth child. She still loves Jacob but she surrenders, at least for now, the dream that her sons will inspire Jacob to love her. In naming the son "Judah," she thanks God for the very first time for her blessings, and thus she comes into her own. After much suffering she has taught herself to focus on the blessings she has rather than aching for what she lacks.

With each baby Leah produces her status in the family is enhanced, but Rachel's self-confidence and self-esteem diminish. With no children to care for at a time when women, lacking the professional or social outlets available to women today, are valued mostly as mothers, Rachel defines her self-worth solely through her competition with Leah. Finally, resentful and bitter, we hear her anguished shrieking out to Jacob, "Give me children or I shall die!" Rachel is not threatening suicide. In her frustration she is crying out for help, hoping to win empathy and understanding from her husband.

Jacob would do anything for Rachel, but her one wish is beyond his power. We can assume that this is not the only time she vents her feelings; rage like this rarely comes out of nowhere. As years pass and her womb remains empty, Jacob has probably learned to dread the monthly burden of Rachel's disappointment. He cares for her deeply but cannot solve her problem. Jacob is also frustrated that Rachel has changed "the terms of the deal." Her role in his life is to charm and entice—not to badger and blame. Like his grandfather Abraham, who grew impatient with the rancor between Sarah and Hagar, Jacob responds to her pain by going on the offensive, feeling disparaged by Rachel and guilty that he has failed in his duty to father her child.

Rachel makes a dangerous mistake when she issues an ultimatum in a futile attempt to draw attention to her misery. Jacob retaliates by implying that God is punishing Rachel. Cruelly, he lashes out, "Can I take the place of God who has denied you fruit of the womb?" What Jacob conveys to Rachel with those callous words is that "God has denied you children; God has not denied *me!*"

Infertility is a recurrent motif in the Bible and husbands fail to understand the pain it inflicts on their wives. The Bible records that hundreds of years after Rachel, in the hill country of Ephraim, Hannah is the favorite of her husband, Elkanah. Like Rachel she is childless for many years. Her bitterness is made all the worse by the second wife, the fertile Peninnah, who keeps taunting her about her barrenness and is jealous of Elkanah's love for Hannah. Sarah was humiliated by Hagar, Rachel by Leah, and Hannah by Peninnah. No husband can put himself in his wife's shoes or understand her pain fully. The matriarchs' husbands' passion for them is insufficient to compensate for the women's unfulfilled longing for children. When Sarah rages because of Hagar, Abraham bolts the tent.

When Rachel cries out in her pain, Jacob's outburst is harsh and impatient. When Elkanah sees that Hannah "wept and would not eat" because his second wife taunts her, his response is tender but focused entirely on his own feelings instead of validating Hannah's anguish. He wonders aloud, "Hannah, why are you crying and why aren't you eating? Am I not more devoted to you than ten sons?" He means well but he does not "get it." The husbands have the best of both worlds—one wife for bearing children and the other for emotional and sexual companionship. The women are left to their own devices to wrestle with their pain and frustration. Finally Sarah gives birth to Isaac, Rachel to Joseph, and Hannah to Samuel. All three sons born to once-barren women become leaders in ancient Israel. It seems the infants were a blessing worth waiting for.

AFTER MANY YEARS JACOB BECOMES a commodity to be traded between his women.

"Once, at the time of the wheat harvest, Reuben came upon some mandrakes in the field and brought them to his mother, Leah. Rachel said to Leah, 'Please give me some of your son's mandrakes.' But she said to her, 'Was it not enough for you to take away my husband that you would also take my son's mandrakes?' Rachel replied, 'I promise, he shall lie with you tonight in return for your son's mandrakes.' When Jacob came home from the field in the evening Leah went out to meet him and said, 'You are to sleep with me for I have hired you with my son's mandrakes.' And he lay with her that night. God heeded Leah and she conceived and bore him a fifth son."

Mandrakes are regarded as potent aphrodisiacs and Rachel wants them to stoke Jacob's passion—and perhaps hers—as well as to reverse her infertility. Leah trades the much-valued tubers and reproaches Rachel for "stealing" Jacob's love. Leah never recovers from her unreciprocated longing for her husband. She conveniently forgets both Laban's role in the scheme and Rachel's prior claim on their beleaguered spouse. In exchange for the mandrakes Rachel "sells" Leah a night with Jacob. With this barter, Rachel confidently demonstrates that she controls who sleeps with Jacob, while Leah, pleased with the trade, expresses no resentment toward this power play. In the evening, as dusk falls, Leah marches out to meet her husband, returning home after a day's work in the fields, and announces boldly, "I have hired you with my son's mandrakes." He follows her obediently, perhaps wordlessly, and she closes the tent flaps behind them.

While it is popular to decry the powerlessness of women in the Bible, it is clear that Jacob's wives pull the strings. The brisk commercial exchange between the sisters is revealing. Rachel and Leah may each want what the other has, but they are also pragmatic about the sexual responsibilities of being a wife in a culture where polygamy is the norm. At the sisters' bidding their maidservants cohabit with Jacob: Bilhah, when Rachel asks her to serve as a surrogate "that through her I too may have children," and Zilpah, at Leah's behest when her body needs a rest from childbearing. Both maidservants have been given by Laban as wedding presents to his daughters. According to the laws of their day, the maidservants are Leah and Rachel's property only—as Hagar was Sarah's. Through years of familiarity and necessity, Rachel and Leah learn to live with their situation. Coolly, Jacob's wives determine with whom their husband spends his nights. Each concubine bears Jacob two sons.

The mandrake episode offers subtle irony and exposes the tension in the triangular relationship. Ensconced with the husband she hires for the night, Leah conceives, but Rachel, clutching a pile of wilting aphrodisiacs, does not. Only after Leah produces two more sons and a daughter, Dina, does "God remember Rachel," opening her womb at last. (The word "remember" reflects the biblical idea of conception as having a profound spiritual dimension.) When Rachel gives birth to a son, her words reveal her innermost feelings: "God has taken away my disgrace." She names the baby Joseph, which in Hebrew means "May God add more." As with Leah's offspring, the child's name tells us about Rachel's longings and yearnings. No sooner does she give birth to the long-awaited son than she is already hoping and praying for the next son. She is never at peace. Barely recovered from the birth of Joseph, she feels obligated to give birth to yet more children.

THROUGH TWENTY YEARS JACOB HAS unconsciously replicated the divisions in his parents' household, allowing his family to become increasingly polarized. He is unable to disrupt the pattern that splits his family into factions and helps foster a climate of contention. The Bible presents all of this as part of the fabric of Jacob's life. His family life is far from ideal, but then as now, the head of a family could devote only part of his attention to personal matters. As Jacob and his wives carry on in this manner over the years, the tension seems to abate, replaced by a sense of resignation and acceptance. But then new circumstances arise that will provide a new focal point for family collaboration.

Jacob is now spiritually primed to return to the land of his parents and take up the mantle of leadership for the third generation. He also hopes to mend his relationship with his twin, Esau.

After twenty years of hard labor, he no longer feels like a usurper and actually feels he has earned his father's blessing.

When Rachel becomes a mother, Jacob is ready to act. He seems to view the birth of Joseph as a turning point, as a signal that the time has come to go back to the Promised Land and to "fear not." He is eager to bring up Rachel's son, Joseph, his favorite, for whom they have waited so long, back in the land of his forebears.

"Jacob put his children and wives on camels and he drove off all his livestock and all the wealth that he had amassed, the livestock in his possession that he had acquired in Paddan-aram, to go to his father Isaac in the land of Canaan. Meanwhile Laban had gone to shear his sheep and Rachel stole her father's household idols. Jacob kept Laban the Aramean in the dark, not telling him that he was fleeing, and fled with all that he had."

Jacob's wives support his decision to return to the land of his birth. Perhaps they think that life in a new country, without their father and brothers nearby, will give them a chance to make a new start on their own terms. Perhaps Rachel has softened now that she too has a child and feels on a more equal footing with her sister. She sets aside her rancor toward Leah and takes the lead in siding with Jacob against their father.

Unbeknownst to Jacob, Rachel steals her father's precious household idols, believed to have powers that protect their owners. Perhaps, unlike her tough-minded Aunt Rebecca, who bolted from her family without looking back, Rachel wants to keep something comforting and familiar from her parental home. Or perhaps she has not given up all the beliefs she has practiced since childhood—a sort of insurance policy. Or it might be that stealing Laban's idols is an attempt to break her father's belief in idols as a first step toward teaching him about the God of Abraham, Isaac, Sarah, and Rebecca. Or perhaps Rachel is prompted by anger. She recalls the humiliation and shame she felt when her father Laban unexpectedly replaced her with Leah in Jacob's bed. The Bible offers no explanation for her theft, nor does it say what becomes of the idols.

Three days after Jacob leaves for Canaan, Laban overtakes his caravan. He accuses Jacob of sneaking off, taking his daughters "like captives of the sword." He also insists that Jacob return the idols, about which Jacob knows nothing. Laban's bellicose demands are the last straw. With Leah and Rachel at his side, Jacob throws off his meek demeanor; his resentment toward Laban for decades of shabby treatment boils over.

"These twenty years I spent in your service, your ewes and she-goats never miscarried nor did I feast on rams from your flock," Jacob tells Laban. "That which was torn by beasts I never brought to you; I myself made good the loss; you exacted it from me, whether snatched by day or snatched by night. Often, scorching heat ravaged me by day and frost by night; and sleep fled from my eyes. Of the twenty years that I spent in your household, I served you fourteen years for your two daughters, and six years for your flocks; and you changed my wages time and again. Had not the God of my father, the God of Abraham and the fear of Isaac, been with me, you would have sent me away empty-handed. But God took notice of my plight and the toil of my hands and gave me judgment last night."

Nevertheless, Laban and Jacob part ways on a civil note. Laban understands that it is impossible for him to persuade Jacob and his daughters to turn back. It is then that Laban "remembers" God's warning: "Beware of attempting anything with Jacob, good or bad."

Jacob and his wives, sons, "cattle, asses, sheep, and male and female slaves" resume their long trek to Canaan.

AS JACOB AND HIS FAMILY continue on their return to his homeland, he dreads the inevitable encounter with his twin, Esau, who has grown powerful and might still be primed for vengeance. Jacob sends his messenger ahead and learns that Esau is coming to meet him at the head of something resembling an army. That Esau is accompanied by four hundred men does not augur well for a peaceful reunion.

Jacob first sends waves of lavish gifts ahead to win Esau's favor, then he, his two wives, his two concubines, and his eleven children cross the ford of the Jabbok River, followed by all his possessions. Vigilantly, he arranges his family in a defensive formation, placing Rachel and Joseph at the end of the long caravan, where they will be safer if Esau attacks. "He divided the children among Leah, Rachel, and the two maids, putting the maids and their children first, Leah and her children next, and Rachel and Joseph last." One can only surmise the deep hurt that Leah's children feel at the blatant favoritism their father shows Rachel and her son. The two sisters find a way of accommodating each other, but Jacob, treasuring Rachel, remains blind to the harm he causes by the privileges he showers on her and her son as he prepares to face his problematic twin. Their resentment will spill over to the next generation, as Leah's sons become bitter rivals to their half-brother, Joseph.

Esau runs to greet Jacob, embraces and kisses him. They reconcile, but Jacob, cautious and wary as always, elects to move his family to a comfortable distance from Esau. Finally, like Isaac and Ishmael before them, Jacob and Esau will come together to bury their father, "gathered to his kin in ripe old age." Thus reconciliation will take place in both generations.

JACOB AND HIS FAMILY RESUME their journey. "They set out from Bethel but when they are still some distance short of Ephrath Rachel was in childbirth and she had hard labor. When her labor was at its hardest the midwife said to her, 'Have no fear for it is another boy for you.' But as she breathed her last—for she was dying—she named him Ben-oni ('son of my suffering'); but his father called him Benjamin," possibly meaning "the son of my right arm."

The caravan halts along a hot, dusty road in search of water to cool Rachel's brow. The women banish Jacob and Joseph from her tent and listen anxiously as Rachel's cries grow weaker through her prolonged labor. The midwife's assurance of "another boy for you" suggests a breach birth, with the baby emerging feet first. As the child she yearned for enters the world, Rachel breathes her last. She seems more concerned with the new life she has created than with her own, which she is about to lose. The saddest memory in the saga of the patriarchal family is Rachel dying while giving birth to her second son on the side of the highway on the way to Bethlehem.

Jacob would have been happy to devote himself to one wife, as Abraham and Isaac before him, but fate dealt him a different hand. He fulfills his conjugal responsibilities to Leah while yearning for Rachel. She is beautiful and melancholy and Jacob is ever in her thrall. As the role of wife has been so ably filled by her earth-mother sister, in Jacob's imagination Rachel is cast in the role of the mistress. Like other biblical women who are barren or have few children, Rachel seems to be the favorite wife who is always sexually and emotionally available to her passionate spouse. Her body is spared the rigors of repeated childbearing and nursing and she remains trim and satisfyingly taut. In fact, one can surmise that Jacob has sex with Leah but with Rachel he makes love. If Rachel loves Jacob she never reveals it. She grows increasingly dissatisfied with Jacob's passion for her. She yearns to get off the pedestal he has put her on and be surrounded with swarms of children like her sister and the other women of the tribe. While Jacob is fulfilled, Rachel is a symbol of the unrequieted yearnings of a life cut down in its prime. After falling in love with her Jacob must wait seven years for her. When his veiled bride turns out to be Leah he has to wait for seven more days to wed Rachel. Then Rachel watches Leah produce sons one after the other until she herself finally gives birth to just one. After Rachel is delivered at last of the second son she yearns for, she dies in childbirth.

Jacob buries Rachel just off the road to Ephrath, now Bethlehem, only one or two days away by caravan from Hebron and the cave of Machpelah. The Bible says nothing of his grief, nor does it explain his haste in burying her. Presumably hot weather necessitates a quick burial, a Jewish tradition to this day. Of all the matriarchs, Rachel alone does not rest in the Cave of the Machpelah, the burial site that Abraham purchased for Sarah and where Rebecca and Leah are buried. Hundreds of years later Rachel remains solitary, watching over the highway as the Children of Israel are forced to leave their Promised Land to go into exile in Babylonia. The prophet Jeremiah, who lived in Jerusalem in 587 BCE and saw the city conquered by Babylonia and its people taken into captivity, will lament

> *A cry is heard in Ramah—*
> *Wailing, bitter weeping—*
> *Rachel weeping for her children.*
> *She refuses to be comforted*
> *For her children, who are gone.*

Jeremiah captures Rachel's enduring melancholy; even in her grave "she refuses to be comforted" as her children are driven into exile.

Jeremiah's lament is further echoed many centuries later by Herman Melville, who ends his masterpiece, *Moby-Dick*, with the words of the sailor Ishmael: "On the second day, a sail drew near, nearer, and picked me up at last. It was the devious-cruising *Rachel*, that in her retracing search after her missing children, only found another orphan."

Rachel's plight—always yearning, never fulfilled—evidently strikes a chord with many throughout the ages. Even today, barren women go to pray for a child at "Rachel's tomb" outside Bethlehem.

Rachel never feels worthy, never feels she has done enough. If only she could have developed some perspective on the gifts in her life, rather than focusing on what she did not have but dreamed of. She might have enjoyed the fact that Jacob loved her till the end of his life, that she did, finally, become pregnant, not just once but twice. It would have been helpful for her to remember Sarah, to turn to the founding mother as a role model: Sarah spent long, devoted years with Abraham without children, and she took pride in her role as a principal of the Covenant.

Rachel's story suggests that we need to give up expectations when it is impossible to fulfill them. Rachel wants to have Jacob's firstborn son; she wants his undivided attention; she wants to bear many children to ensure her part in the founding of a great nation, as the Covenant promises. None of this is to be. She is resentful of her sister. She is frustrated and angry with Jacob. She does not, however, blame God. Ultimately, she learns to make compromises with Leah so that daily life is bearable and perhaps at moments even sweet. Sometimes this is the best we can hope for, and we should be grateful to achieve even that.

The vision of romantic melancholy expressed by Jeremiah, rather than what Rachel does or says in the biblical Book of Genesis, secures her popular veneration to this day. She symbolizes the loving mother who sacrifices her life for her child. She is the romantic figure whose life is cut short before she can achieve her full potential as a matriarch equal to her sister.

She does not live to see her sons Joseph and Benjamin grow up, yet her brief life helps to shape history. Joseph, born of semi-nomadic shepherds, rises to become the indispensable adviser to Pharaoh. He ensures that Jacob's other sons, his half-brothers, survive a famine in Canaan when they seek succor in Egypt, the breadbasket of the ancient world. He is the leader in the family who brings about forgiveness, after an admittedly long process, which will end the painful feud among the great-grandchildren of Abraham and Sarah.

Jacob, Rachel, and Leah are dealt a set of circumstances that present intensely difficult challenges. Marriage, love, sex, and childbirth all pull them in different directions, and the new faith in the One God hangs on a slender thread as its followers are vulnerable to attack, war, and absorption into the surrounding pagan cultures. The competition to produce more children is not merely a facet of the rivalry between Jacob's sibling wives but also reflects their concern with ensuring the continuity of their small seminomadic tribe of shepherds at this early stage of their new faith.

The wives of Jacob, like all the matriarchs in the Book of Genesis, are united with their husbands by a single focus: their shared dedication to the survival and continuity of their faith and way of life. They are not saints but pilgrims on a journey. In every case, a purpose-driven life forces them to set aside their personal conflicts to sustain the family as a cohesive unit and the means of preserving their identity and people.

ONE HOPES THAT AFTER RACHEL'S death Leah enjoyed some tranquil years with her husband. Jealousy and competition would have been a thing of the past. Although Jacob loved Leah less than Rachel, Leah gave birth to ten of his twelve sons, as well as their daughter, Dina. Leah reigns supreme as the mother of Israel's tribes: her name is cited as a revered source of blessing along with the names of Sarah, Rebecca, and Rachel—the strong, steadfast mothers of a new people.

But Leah's name is always mentioned after Rachel's. In the memory of the Jewish people, Rachel has remained a unique, romantic figure. She is Jacob's first, last, and only love.

FIVE

THE WIDOW WHO DARED

T O TAKE CONTROL OF HER destiny, the young widow Tamar plots an audacious scheme that defies the patriarchal order of her time.

Leah and Jacob's fourth son, Judah, has married and the woman bears him three sons, Er, Onan, and Shelah. The eldest, Er, marries Tamar, also a Canaanite. When Er dies suddenly, Judah observes the custom known as the levirate law—from the Latin word *levir*, meaning "brother-in-law"—which obligates a brother to marry the widow of his brother if he dies without male issue. The purpose, as defined in Deuteronomy, is "that the first son she bears shall be accounted to the dead brother that his name may not be blotted out in Israel."

We read that Leah and Jacob's son has married a Canaanite woman. In the time of Abraham and Isaac, it was important for the patriarchs to marry within their kin because the new faith was fragile, confined to a small clan, and often consisted of a personal dialogue between them and God. By the time Judah is a grown man and leader, the new faith is more established and secure, and the fathers of the twelve tribes of Israel are in place.

Judah instructs Onan, his second son, " 'Join with your brother's wife and do your duty by her as a brother-in-law, and provide offspring for your brother.' But Onan, knowing that the seed would not count as his, let it go to waste whenever he joined with his brother's wife, so as not to provide heirs for his brother. What he did was displeasing to the Lord and He took his life also." The spare account of Onan's visits glosses over the intimate encounters that must have been degrading and frustrating to Tamar.

To Onan, the levirate law is unfair. The death of his older brother opens the way for him to assume the considerable rights and privileges of the firstborn son. Instead, the law compels him to father the child who will sustain his brother's name and birthright and block his sons from inheritance.

Onan, resentful as he enters Tamar's home, responds against his will to the charms of the attractive woman his brother loved. When he "joins with her," his passion cannot be denied, but at the last moment he withdraws, wasting his seed on the ground.

Again and again Tamar steels herself to endure his visits. One presumes that she gives her own pleasure no more thought than Onan does, but she summons all of the lovemaking skills she honed with her first husband, hoping that Onan will fully consummate their union. If she conceives, she tells herself, she will forgo the anger that surges through her each time she subjects herself to Onan's rough, impersonal touch. But Onan makes certain not to plant his seed in Tamar.

Onan's birth control method, coitus interruptus, known today as withdrawal, "was displeasing to the Lord." Not only does Onan repudiate his legal duty to Tamar, but in doing so he fails to sire the children so essential to the continuation of his clan.

Tamar is determined to honor the ways of her husband's people and to remain part of his family. Because he does not share her commitment, Onan pays the ultimate price and dies for his refusal.

It now falls on Judah's youngest son, Shelah, to ensure that the eldest brother's line continues. Judah orders Tamar to return to her father's house and to live there as a widow until the boy Shelah is old enough to marry her.

Judah, however, does not intend to keep his promise to Tamar and fulfill the law. Two of his sons shared her bed, he thinks, and now both are dead. Judah fears that if his last son, Shelah, marries or beds Tamar, "he too might die like his brothers."

Tamar seethes with injured pride but must repress her rage. She longs to bear a child, yet she is denied any opportunity for conceiving. As a childless widow in her father's house, she is an unwanted burden with no economic or social standing. She is isolated and lonely. The biblical narrator mentions no mother, sister, friend, or kinsman who might comfort her or speak on her behalf. Moreover, she is now considered a foreigner in her own community.

Tamar, wearing the black garb of a widow and living the chaste life of a spinster, sees her childbearing years slip away.

Years pass and Judah's wife dies. Shelah comes of age. Well versed in her rights under levirate law, Tamar knows Judah is obliged to marry her to Shelah, the remaining brother, but after years of neglect and procrastination, she understands that this marriage will never take place. She believes confronting Judah will be useless. He knows what his responsibilities are, and after trying to fulfill them, with a disastrous outcome, he has backed away from the levirate law and from her. She further knows that she, universally viewed as a "contaminated" widow whose first two husbands died, is a poor candidate for remarriage—a woman who bears a curse.

Her standing in the community depends entirely upon her role as a wife and mother. Over the years, through endless chores and lonely nights, she has thought through the only two choices left to her. She can be humble and be obsequious and remain in her father's house for the rest of her life. Or she can take action, using her intelligence, courage, and the power of sex to create the future to which she feels entitled. She is painfully conscious of the narrow window of time during which she will be able to conceive a child.

Tamar resolves not to be cast aside. She devises a plan and waits for the right opportunity. When she hears that Judah is en route to Timnah for the sheepshearing, she is prepared. Her scheme is bold and dangerous, but she has gathered all the information she needs. She knows that during the celebrations that mark the sheepshearing season, many men enjoy the services of harlots who set up shop at the roadside. She assumes that Judah, a recent widower, is likely to be open to an offer of sex.

But what if someone other than Judah approaches her? What if it is not the right time of the month for her to conceive? What if Judah does not show up or chooses another route? What if someone denounces her as a harlot? She is willing to take these risks.

Tamar makes her way to Enaim and selects a spot at the cross-road where Judah will surely see her as he travels to Timnah. Known in Hebrew as "the mother of the roads," a crossroad is a timeless metaphor for a crucial decision.

With the fluid grace of a dancer, she transforms herself, quickly covering her face with a veil and wrapping herself in its gauzy billows. Her position by the road advertises her profession. Who but a harlot would dare sit alone alongside a public thoroughfare?

The Bible records that Tamar "sat down at the entrance to Enaim, which is on the road to Timnah. When Judah saw her, he took her for a harlot; for she had covered her face. So he turned aside to her by the road and said, 'Here, let me sleep with you'— for he did not know that she was his daughter-in-law.

" 'What,' she asked, 'will you pay for sleeping with me?'

"He replied, 'I will send a kid from my flock.'

"But she said, 'You must leave a pledge until you have sent it.'

"And he said, 'What pledge shall I give you?'

"She replied, 'Your seal and cord and the staff which you carry.'

"So he gave them to her and lay with her and she conceived by him. Then she went on her way. She took off her veil and again put on her widow's garb."

The transaction is straightforward, businesslike. There are no titillating or erotic details. We know only that the encounter lasts long enough for her to conceive a child before Judah continues his journey. As Tamar quickly departs from the scene of seduction, she removes her veil, resumes the role of the widow, and hopes that no one but Judah knows what happened.

An honorable man, Judah attempts to redeem his pledge. He

sends a trusted friend, the Adullamite named Hirah, to find the woman, deliver the goat he promised, and redeem the tokens of his pledge. Judah is puzzled and alarmed when Hirah reports that not only has the woman vanished but no one remembers seeing a harlot at the location Judah identified. Judah worries that others might recognize his seal and spread reports that he visited a prostitute, bringing shame to him among the members of his tribe. Eager to avoid such gossip, he decides to stop searching for the harlot and put the matter behind him.

As the months pass, Tamar can no longer conceal her swelling belly from public view. Judah learns that Tamar is with child when sneering townspeople inform him, "Your daughter-in-law played the harlot; in fact, she is with child by harlotry." Judah rushes to judgment, demanding, "Bring her out . . . and let her be burned."

Tamar is well aware that the punishment for conceiving a child out of wedlock is death. As she steps forward, alone in the world except for the child growing within her, a mob of villagers surrounds her, relishing her disgrace.

Tamar stands erect like the date palm for which she is named. She is calm, confident that her cause is just. She needs only a few words to describe her situation to Judah. As she is brought out, she hands her father-in-law a parcel and a message: " 'I am with child by the man to whom these belong.' And she added, 'Examine these; whose seal and cord and staff are these?' "

The suspense reaches a climax as Tamar stands all by herself, head held high, facing the powerful patriarch Judah in the midst of the jeering, bloodthirsty villagers. She does not know if her courage will pay off or whether she, along with her unborn child, will be burned alive.

Confronted with the artifacts, Judah retreats from his hasty condemnation of his daughter-in-law's alleged harlotry. He recognizes the items in the parcel as his own and what they mean. He must acknowledge Tamar's claim of his paternity or let her and his heir be killed unjustly. Even though Tamar misled him at the Enaim-Timnah crossroad and now exposes him to public shame, Judah draws on his best character traits—decency and righteousness—in an act that presages the Israelite leader he will become. He does not deny the truth, make excuses, or point to Tamar as a scapegoat. Rather he takes responsibility and blames himself. He had disregarded the law by not providing for Tamar, and he had disregarded his family obligations by sending her away from the family.

He declares, "She is more right than I, inasmuch as I did not give her to my son Shelah." The villagers are astounded; the mob disperses.

Judah welcomes Tamar back into his family. But, the Bible flatly notes, he and Tamar are never sexually intimate again: "he knew her again no more." Six months later Tamar gives birth to twin boys, Perez and Zerah. Not only is she not punished, but the newborns ensure the future of what will become the tribe of Judah and establish the ancestral line leading to King David centuries later, and later still, according to Christian tradition, to Jesus.

THE ESSENCE OF TAMAR'S STORY is that she refuses to crawl into a dark corner of her father's house and disappear. Though apparently powerless, she does not allow Judah to ignore her legal rights. Tamar's father-in-law shows his upright spirit by acknowledging that he has misused her.

Ultimately both Tamar and Judah choose the high road.

Tamar boldly maneuvers to escape two tragedies: the private misery of lonely, childless widowhood and the public execution of a woman who refused to accept such a fate.

Judah is a co-beneficiary of her scheme, because her willingness to "play the harlot" ensures the continuation of his line. Like Eve, Tamar uses her full sexual power to advance a righteous cause. While we may find it shocking that Tamar tricked her father-in-law into a sexual liaison, her willingness to risk everything to bear a child, no matter how far she had to reach beyond customary social norms, wins her a place in the history of her people. Tamar's drive to conceive a child is indomitable, undeterred even by the threat of death. Her unconventional use of her sexuality challenges the patriarch who had failed to fulfill his legal obligations to her.

Tamar has no wish to humiliate Judah. By handing him the parcel with his seal, cord, and staff, she gives him the opportunity to own up to what he did and to act as a wise judge and humble leader. Eventually Jacob, his father, singles Judah out as the leader of his brothers and predicts that "the scepter shall not depart from Judah" and "the homage of peoples" will be his.

In their quest to have a child, many modern women defy social conventions or push the limits of biology and technology. Of course, they do not face the particular set of social and traditional obstacles confronting Tamar. Today's women have multiple options that were unavailable to her, including remarriage, adoption, and high-tech fertilization techniques. But the values the Bible celebrates in this story—personal courage and a woman's irrepressible drive to create new life—are timeless.

It is not enough, however, merely to dream about changing the status quo and hope for better times. Tamar, passionate about bearing a child, refuses to wallow in self-pity or to accept the injustice dealt her. She does her homework, keeps her focus on her goals, and thinks creatively and constructively about how to achieve them. Her boldness, fearlessness, and resilience produce what she ultimately desires: the position of a respected matriarch in her dead husband's family.

The biblical scribes treat Tamar's resourcefulness and defiance of convention with dignity and sympathy. Her story affirms that a single human being is able to make a profound difference to history, even if that person is "only a woman," an outsider, and one of society's least powerful members. Tamar deploys imagination and initiative to control her own destiny rather than waiting for a miracle or resigning herself to perpetual servitude. The Bible lauds and rewards her courage because they serve a goal larger than her own immediate welfare: the preeminent biblical values of family and continuity.

SIX

HOW DELILAH TRAPS
THE MIGHTY SAMSON

SAMSON, THE FOLK HERO OF superhuman strength in the Bible's Book of Judges, is an overgrown adolescent, an impulsive, ill-mannered loner. Living in the twelfth century BCE, Samson and his fellow Israelites are restive under the yoke of the stronger, well-armed Philistines. Samson, however, finds Philistine women irresistible and falls for Delilah, a savvy Philistine spy. This story of desire and betrayal entails a journey from destructive obsession to spiritual insight and final redemption.

Like many mothers of the Bible's outstanding men—including Sarah, Rebecca, Rachel, and Hannah—Samson's mother is barren for many years. The Bible describes how an angel of God appears to her, warning her "not to drink wine or other intoxicant, or to eat anything unclean. For you are going to conceive and bear a son; let no razor touch his head, for the boy is to be a Nazirite to God from the womb on." (The Hebrew word *Nazirite* means someone set apart, defined by a vow—a voluntary act of devotion—such as refraining from cutting one's hair or abstaining from alcohol.) In this case the Nazirite status involves a lofty purpose. The angel says of the promised son: "He shall be the first to deliver Israel from the Philistines."

Curiously, the Bible does not give the mother's name. She reports to her husband, Manoah, her encounter with a man "who looked like an angel of God," and Manoah is elated that they are to have a son. A little later she again meets with the angel while "she was sitting in the field and her husband Manoah was not with her." She goes to tell Manoah, who follows her and finds the angel still sitting in the field. Manoah too hears the prediction and accepts the conditions stipulated for the rearing of his future son.

"And the woman bore a son, and she named him Samson. The boy grew up, and the Lord blessed him." The parents' long stretch of infertility suggests that they are elderly and that they are overwhelmed by the miracle of Samson's birth. Having been told that their son will be the liberator of his people, they are too intimidated to impose the limits that every child needs. Samson grows up with the classic traits of a spoiled, narcissistic child: a grandiose sense of self-importance, a preoccupation with fantasies of unlimited power, exhibitionism, and a thirst for constant admiration. If he ever ponders the implications of the heroic expectations that God and his parents set for him, the Bible does not mention it.

Samson must see that he is different from his peers. He may be teased in his village for being an oversize, long-haired hulk, and perhaps children whisper and tease him about the strange man, said to be an angel, his mother met out in the fields.

Growing up in one of the pastoral, tradition-bound hill villages of the poor, small Israelite tribe of Dan, Samson is drawn to the forbidden world of the enemy: the rich, sophisticated, sexually permissive Philistines who live in the five towns along the Mediterranean seacoast. He is ambivalent about the Philistines. He wants to be accepted among their fun-loving young men; they are intrigued by his physical strength, but they also humiliate him and refuse to treat him as one of their own. Under the surface his resentment seethes.

The Bible tells us that on one occasion Samson visits Timnah, a town in the hill country of Judah, where he notices a girl among the Philistine women. On his return home he tells his parents about her and demands, "Get her for me as a wife." They reply, "Is there no one among the daughters of your own kinsmen and among all our people that you must go and take a wife from the uncircumcised Philistines?"

But Samson pays them no heed. He orders his father, "Get me that one, for she is the one that pleases me." So Samson and his father and mother go to Timnah.

On a previous occasion, when Samson passed through a vineyard in Timnah alone, "a full-grown lion came roaring at him. The spirit of the Lord gripped him and he tore him asunder with his bare hands as one might tear a kid asunder; but he did not tell his father and mother what he had done. Then he went down and spoke to the woman, and she pleased Samson." Samson, taken aback by his own strength, chooses not to tell his parents about the lion. He acts alone, and for the rest of his life he remains a loner.

Only at the end of his life does he cease conducting himself as a willful, self-absorbed adolescent. In some ways he resembles some of our contemporary celebrities: he has extraordinary physical skills and discipline, for which he wins the adulation of his peers and their parents. However, he is focused only on himself and his own desires, which, combined with the willingness of others to do his bidding and tolerate his self-centeredness, leads to his apparent belief that consequences do not apply to him.

Samson's plan to marry a Philistine woman troubles his parents, but they trudge along with their son to Timnah so that Manoah may talk to the woman "who pleased Samson well."

The wedding takes place, but it leads to an escalation of Samson's rage and vengefulness. At the rowdy Philistine bachelor party during the traditional seven-day wedding feast, all are drinking except Samson, who remains wary when in the company of the Philistines and is careful to honor his Nazirite vows. To contribute to the festivities, he invents a riddle based on the honeycomb built by a swarm of bees in the carcass of the lion he slew. He tells his guests that if they solve the riddle before the week is over, he will give them "thirty linen tunics and thirty sets of clothing." If they fail to deliver the right answer by the same deadline, they will have to provide him with thirty linen tunics and thirty sets of clothing. They say to him, "Ask your riddle and we will listen."

Samson's riddle is

> "Out of the eater came something to eat,
> Out of the strong came something sweet."

Samson's wedding guests, not accepting Samson as one of their own, resent his power over them and the conditions he sets before them. They approach his bride in secret, threatening harm to her and her family unless she inveigles Samson into revealing the answer to the riddle. "Then Samson's wife harassed him with tears, and she said, 'You really hate me, you don't love me. You asked my countrymen a riddle, and you didn't tell me the answer.' He replied, 'I haven't even told my father and mother; shall I tell you?' During the rest of the seven days of the feast she continued to harass him with her tears, and on the seventh day he told her, because she nagged him so. She then went and explained the riddle to her countrymen. On the seventh day, before sunset, the townsmen said to him: 'What is sweeter than honey, / And what is stronger than a lion?' "

Samson immediately understands that his bride has betrayed him. Angry and humiliated, he tells his guests: "Had you not plowed with my heifer, / You would not have guessed my riddle!" letting them know that he understands that his guests have gleaned the information from his wife. "Heifer" refers to his wife, and "plowing" suggests sexual intimacy between the Philistines and his Philistine bride.

Samson's revenge is brutal. "The spirit of the Lord gripped him. He went down to Ashkelon and killed thirty of its [Philistine] men. He stripped them and gave the sets of clothing to those who had answered the riddle." Still in a rage, Samson leaves for his father's house, apparently abandoning his wife, whose father then marries her off to one of the wedding guests.

Time passes, and Samson decides to visit his wife and is enraged to discover that she has been married off to someone else. Attempting to calm him down, her father suggests that he marry her younger sister, who, he says, is "more beautiful than" the former wife. Samson feels his rights have been violated. He declares, "Now the Philistines can have no claim against me for the harm I shall do them."

Samson's vengeance has the exaggerated tenor of a folktale, as does the rest of his story. He catches three hundred foxes, pairs them, and places a burning torch between the tails of each pair. Then he turns the foxes "loose among the standing grain of the Philistines, setting fire to stacked grain, standing grain, vineyards, and olive trees." The Philistine villagers, furious with Samson, attack his ex-wife from Timnah along with her father and burn them alive.

The Philistines then resolve to capture Samson himself.

He is fearless as a fighter but hopelessly naïve when it comes to women. Though he battles the Philistines, killing a thousand men on one occasion, he cannot keep away from their women.

The Philistines see their opportunity in Samson's frequent visits to the red-light districts of Ashkelon, Gaza, and other Philistine cities. They discover that Samson "loves" Delilah, a Philistine informant in the Valley Sorek. Their leaders approach the woman and offer a lucrative deal: "Coax him and find out what makes him so strong and how we can overpower him, tie him up, and make him helpless; and we'll each give you eleven hundred shekels of silver."

Her voice dripping with honey, Delilah asks Samson, " 'Tell me, what makes you so strong? And how could you be tied up and made helpless?' Samson replied, 'If I were to be tied with seven fresh tendons that had not been dried, I should become as weak as an ordinary man.' So the lords of the Philistines brought up to her seven fresh tendons that had not been dried. She bound him with them while an ambush was waiting in her room. Then she called

out to him, 'Samson, the Philistines are upon you!' Whereat he
pulled the tendons apart as a strand of tow comes apart at the touch
of fire. So the secret of this strength remained unknown."

Apparently having learned his lesson after his experience with
his wife and his riddle, Samson is careful not to let down his guard
and reveal the source of his strength. But Delilah, shrewd and ve-
nal, knows that he is enthralled with her, and she is confident that
she can somehow worm his secret out of him.

Samson is attracted to Delilah for many of the same reasons
that have drawn him to Philistines in general. They are different
from his fellow Israelites, and their seemingly superior "other-
ness"—their political, technological, and military might, a life free
from many of the strictures of his faith—fascinate him.

As Delilah flatters and cajoles him, her questions about help-
lessness suggest a new erotic component in their nightly encounters
that Samson finds he cannot live without. They quickly establish the
terms of bondage. Each night he describes a set of restraints and
says that if she employs them to tie him up, he "would become as
weak as an ordinary man." Then Delilah binds him and summons
the Philistines, crying out, "Samson, the Philistines are upon you!"
Samson flexes his muscles and the restraints snap off like threads.
The next night, her voice husky with admiration, she again insists,
"Do tell me how you could be tied up."

Samson becomes obsessed with Delilah, losing control of
himself, the sense of who he is, where his loyalties lie, and indeed,
any caution for self-preservation. The game he is addicted to is
dangerous. With reckless self-confidence he gambles away his life,
his people's future, and God's plan. He cares about one thing only:
satisfying his sexual craving.

Delilah pouts and taunts him: "How can you say you love me, when you don't confide in me? This makes three times that you've deceived me and haven't told me what makes you so strong."

Samson's resolve to keep his secret weakens. "Finally, after she had nagged him and pressed him constantly, he was wearied to death and he confided everything to her. He said to her, 'No razor has ever touched my head, for I have been a Nazirite to God since I was in my mother's womb. If my hair were cut, my strength would leave me and I should become as weak as an ordinary man.'"

Delilah senses that this time, with an answer so different from the previous ones, Samson has told her the truth. She lulls Samson to sleep while the Philistine leaders wait anxiously in the shadows with "the eleven hundred shekels of silver" each has promised her. His muscular body rests in the soft, yielding flesh of Delilah's lap. He is as trusting as a child. He deludes himself into believing that her love is as deep as his.

On her cue a leader of the Philistines comes into the chamber, cuts off seven locks of Samson's hair, and leaves. Then the nightly routine resumes with Delilah crying out, "Samson, the Philistines are upon you!"

Waking, Samson thinks that he will break loose and shake himself free as usual. But as the biblical text notes, "he did not know that the Lord had departed from him."

As he raises his hand to touch his hair, he recognizes Delilah's betrayal and his own degradation. Without his hair Samson is as weak as any other human being.

With the pieces of silver in her hand, Delilah is finally silent. She stands by as the Philistines seize her paramour and gouge out his eyes. They shackle him in bronze fetters and make him a slave, turning a mill in the prison.

By sharing the secret of his God-given gift, Samson has sold the equivalent of his birthright for fleeting moments of pleasure, just as Jacob's twin brother Esau once traded his birthright for a bowl of lentils. In both cases the desire for instant gratification barred the way to a brilliant future. Throughout history we know of powerful men who, like Samson, have entered sexual liaisons that compromised everything they worked for all their lives.

Unbeknownst to Samson, however, he is to be given a second chance. "After his hair was cut off, it began to grow back."

Time passes. The Philistines, still rejoicing over Samson's capture, gather in their main temple to offer a sacrifice to their god Dagon. "As their spirits rose, they said, 'Call Samson here and let him dance for us.' Samson was fetched from the prison and he danced for them."

The skin of his ankles rubbed raw by the heavy shackles, Samson is forced to perform like a circus bear for the jeering crowd. The sockets of his eyes are dark and empty. But paradoxically, he now sees with a clarity that eluded him in the days of his superhuman strength, when his passion for Delilah blinded him. His life was about heroics rather than true heroism, which demands sacrifice. His own enslavement and humiliation now mirror the oppression of his people under Philistine rule.

The Philistines place Samson between the pillars of their great temple. "Samson said to the boy who was leading him by the hand, 'Let go of me and let me feel the pillars that the temple rests on, that I may lean on them.' Now the temple was full of men and women; all the lords of the Philistines were there, and there were some three thousand men and women on the roof watching Samson dance."

As they mock him, he understands the true source of his

power. His thick tresses now grown back, the spirit of God returns to him. Samson calls out, " 'O Lord God! Please remember me and give me strength just this once, O God, to take revenge of the Philistines, if only for one of my two eyes.' He embraced the two middle pillars that the temple rested upon, one with his right arm and one with his left, and leaned against them; Samson cried, 'Let me die with the Philistines!' and he pulled with all his might. The temple came crashing down on the lords and on all the people in it. Those that were slain by him as he died outnumbered those who had been slain by him when he lived."

With their leaders dead, the Philistines scatter and are soon vanquished by the Israelites.

Samson's kinsmen dig through the rubble of the temple to find the body of their fallen hero. Then "his brothers and all his father's household came down and carried him up and buried him in the tomb of his father Manoah, between the villages of Zorah and Eshtaol." Thus Samson returns to his roots, the place from which he came, for "the spirit of the Lord first moved him in the encampment of Dan," between the villages of Zorah and Eshtaol. Samson, who spent much of his life among the Philistines, returned with honor to the land of his birth; to the tribe of Dan.

ONE OF THE BIBLE'S BEST-KNOWN stories, Samson's affair with Delilah has been depicted again and again in folktales and novels, in art, opera, and film. The theme is usually the contrast between a lonely, unreflecting giant's superhuman strength and a sophisticated woman's cunning in reducing him to powerlessness. As a celebrity famous only for his physical prowess, Samson might not have gained himself a place in biblical lore. But with his last conscious act, Samson is transformed into a hero and his daredevil exploits enter the history of his people.

Naïve, trusting, and unable to learn from past experience, Samson falls twice for Philistine women who betray him to their fellow countrymen. To his parents and his tribe, these women represent a threat and cannot be trusted. But the muscle-bound strongman, the would-be rescuer of his oppressed people, is putty in their hands. Their nagging and weeping reduces Samson to a weakling, a fool, and a moral coward.

Once he is captured and enslaved, Samson's options are limited. One is to beg God to set him free or help him escape. Another is to take his own life. A third is to endure imprisonment and, presumably, eventual death at the hands of his captors. But in all these cases he would fail to make good the prophecy and "deliver Israel from the Philistines." Samson finds a way to end his life for the benefit of his people. By choosing to sacrifice himself for the greater good, Samson gives meaning to his death and leaves a legacy of heroism to the Israelite tribes.

Samson's last lonely feat occurs after he comes to understand that the extraordinary strength he squandered and abused most of his life was a gift from God. Only when he is taunted and reviled as a slave in a pagan temple does he draw close to his God, for the very first time crying out to Him for help as he walks "through the valley of the shadow of death." Now that he is blind, he "sees" for the very first time. At the moment that he seems physically the weakest, he is spiritually the strongest.

Samson is a fatally flawed character—problematic, even maddening. His fabulous displays of strength have gripped people's imagination, yet few parents name their son Samson (or for that matter, few name their daughter Delilah). Modern commentators diagnose a range of emotional and physical disorders that seem to fit this impulsive, sometimes violent young man. Some say that the secret Delilah discovered was sexual masochism, defined in the *Diagnostic and Statistical Manual of Mental Disorders* as "a preferred or exclusive mode of producing sexual excitement, to be humiliated, bound, beaten, or otherwise made to suffer." Others argue that the cutting of Samson's hair symbolizes castration. But such clinical interpretations disparage Samson and rob his story of its tragic triumph.

Delilah's name is usually invoked in popular culture to illustrate how easily a false-hearted woman can bring a strong man to ruin. That is strictly a male perspective that could apply equally to a woman infatuated with a deceptive, sweet-talking man. Rather, Samson is solely responsible for his own reckless behavior, especially after the tragic fate of his Philistine wife. He knows that the Philistines are ruthless people. Blaming Delilah for Samson's fall is similar to blaming Eve for Adam's disobedience in the Garden of Eden. Neither Adam nor Samson is forced into a sexual relationship. Both are free moral agents responsible for the actions they take. Depicting men as weak-kneed victims of female machinations only serves to infantilize them and to deprive them of personal responsibility and accountability.

While Samson falls in love with Delilah, she neither reciprocates nor feels any loyalty toward him, nor does she claim to. She never tells him she loves him, only points out to him that he tells her he loves her but "mocks" her with false answers about the source of his strength. To her, he is a client like any other, though more famous and more valuable. His people are her people's enemy. She is street savvy, an informer on familiar terms with the authorities. She is paid, and paid well, and money is what matters most to her.

A reality check is useful in most emotional relationships, and Samson would have benefited from asking himself the following questions: What is attracting me in this relationship? What am I giving and what am I getting in return? Am I being a victim or merely rebellious? Is there some thrill of the forbidden about the relationship? Am I attempting to gain power over someone—the enemy, my parents, other authority figures—in this relationship? Am I indulging a sense of omniscience or grandiosity—the ability to enter the lion's den and escape unharmed? Have I lost all sense of independence and autonomy?

On the other hand, if Samson had thought about these questions, he probably wouldn't have ended up as a biblical hero and liberated the Israelites from the Philistines.

Unlike other women in the biblical chronicle, Delilah is not identified by any kinship relations. No mention is made of father, husband, or children. Even her ethnic origin goes unmentioned, though we assume she is a Philistine, as she has ties to the lords of the Philistines and lives in the unstable borderland between the Israelites and the Philistines. We know simply that she is a woman from the Valley Sorek and a hardheaded, independent operator with neither the protection nor the restrictions of a patriarchal family structure. The Bible is careful not to humanize her in any way by offering details from her personal life. What she does, she does well—she knows her customer's needs—and she does purely for money. The amount is substantial and suggests that not even feelings of patriotism are involved in the transaction.

Delilah is no hapless streetwalker unsure from one day to the next where her next meal will come from. She is a hard-nosed entrepreneur. In a society where men control all power, women resort to sexual means to survive. (Today women have more options, but we still see women risking their lives to teeter on five-inch high heels so as to appeal to men.) Beguiling, worldly, and misleading, she is irresistible to Samson once she discovers the brand of sexuality he craves. Delilah is the quintessential cold-blooded seductress and temptress, the femme fatale who leads men astray with her sexual power over them. In the power struggle between the two, Delilah wins. Having carried out her assignment, she has nothing to do with Samson's imprisonment and final comeback. The biblical narrator offers only a few terse words about her, relaying only what is necessary to depict Samson's weaknesses; the narrator does not even mention whether she is among the dead at the temple Samson destroys. She is no role model; she offers no wisdom or guidance.

Delilah displays the energetic traits that characterize other women in the Bible stories: she is resourceful and independent of spirit. In her case, however, her strengths are put to service the furtherance of her own greed. Even love of country does not figure into her betrayal of Samson. The contrast between Delilah (and later Jezebel) and the other women in the Bible demonstrates that character can function for good or ill. The difference is motive.

In keeping with its overarching theme of man's free will, however, the Bible does not judge or punish this businesswoman and sex worker of ancient times. God created humans in His own image—that is, with free moral choice—but the expectation is that ensuing decisions will be moral ones. The sparseness of the stories induces readers to engage with the characters and develop their own interpretations of what happened and why. Delilah betrays Samson but she does not misrepresent herself to him. Nonetheless, our sympathy lies with the muscle-bound strongman who, self-deluded, melts in her presence but in the end, tortured and blinded, fulfills his designated role and saves his people.

SEVEN

MICHAL,

DAVID'S FIRST WIFE

AROUND 1050 BCE, MICHAL, KING Saul's younger daughter, is in love with a young shepherd from Bethlehem by the name of David, son of Jesse. Shielded from the harsh realities of life, the princess is smug in her royal status. When Michal first meets David, he is celebrated as a champion of the Israelites. With a sling and a stone, he slew the heavily armored giant Goliath in single combat and saved the kingdom from enslavement by the Philistines. The Bible describes David as "ruddy-cheeked, bright-eyed, and handsome . . . skilled in music . . . a stalwart fellow and a warrior, sensible in speech, and the Lord was with him."

Like many of her fellow Israelites, Michal can repeat from memory David's bold challenge to Goliath: "You come to me with sword and spear and javelin; but I come against you in the name of the Lord of Hosts, the God of the armies of Israel, whom you have defiled . . . and this whole assembly shall know that the Lord can give victory without sword or spear. For the battle is the Lord's, and He will deliver you into our hands."

Like his countrymen, King Saul, the first of Israel's monarchs, is relieved that Goliath is no more and that the Philistines are vanquished. But the more the women sing David's praises, the more Saul becomes distressed. "When the [troops] came home [and] David returned from killing the Philistine, the women of all the towns of Israel came out singing and dancing to greet King Saul with timbrels, shouting, and sistrums. The women sang as they danced, and they chanted:

Saul has slain his thousands;
David his tens of thousands!"

Jealousy gnaws at Saul's soul as he realizes, "To David they have given tens of thousands, and to me they have given thousands. All that he lacks is the kingship!" The following day, the Bible continues, "an evil spirit of God gripped Saul and he began to rave in the house, while David was playing the [lyre], as he did daily. Saul had a spear in his hand, and Saul threw the spear, thinking to pin David to the wall. But David eluded him twice." After this failure to kill David, Saul becomes afraid of him, seeing that God is with David and has "turned away from Saul."

The Bible's first reference to mental illness is graphic. Saul sinks into a deep depression. David's soothing music—an early reference to the use of music as therapy to calm ravaged nerves—fails to ward off Saul's attack.

Saul's next move is to send David to the "head of the troops," hoping that the Philistines will kill him. But "when Saul saw that [David] was successful, he dreaded him." By now, the Bible notes, "all Israel and Judah loved David, for he marched at their head" against the Philistines. Saul, in a tactical shift, then offers David his elder daughter, Merab, in marriage; in return, David is to become the king's warrior and "fight the battles of the Lord." David demurs, citing his lowly origins: "Who am I and what is my life—my father's family in Israel—that I should become Your Majesty's son-in-law?" After David declines his offer, the king abruptly changes his mind and gives Merab in marriage to another man.

Then Michal, King Saul's younger daughter, achieves a rare distinction. The Bible says, "Now Michal daughter of Saul had fallen in love with David." This is the only time the Bible notes that a woman has fallen in love. The wording "Michal daughter of Saul" suggests that her feelings influence the choice of her husband because of her privileged position as princess, whereas with most marriages at that time, the woman's personal feelings were rarely taken into account. The Bible is mute, however, about David's feelings for Michal—either because he had not chosen to express them or because a commoner's feelings were not important. We are left with a vague impression that something is off balance in this relationship.

Michal's love for the young hero fits neatly into the calculations of both Saul and David. "I will give her to him," Saul says, "and she can serve as a snare for him, so that the Philistines may kill him." David makes no pretense at loving or desiring Michal, but after he kills two hundred Philistines, he calculates that marriage into the royal family might prove politically advantageous if he should one day claim the throne. He changes his mind about the disparity in social status and now claims to be pleased by the idea of becoming the king's son-in-law.

In another of his volatile moods, Saul becomes deeply agitated and overwhelmed with terror. "When Saul realized that the Almighty was with David and that Michal daughter of Saul loved him, Saul grew still more afraid of David; and Saul was David's enemy ever after. Saul urged his son Jonathan and all his courtiers to kill David." Instead Jonathan becomes David's lifelong friend and secret ally while the courtiers and their local informants plot to carry out the king's command.

Michal and David are wed. David is preoccupied with building up his reputation and political power while dodging the assassins his father-in-law sends to kill him. For David, love is a luxury he does not expect in a political marriage. But for the princess Michal, with passions and dreams of her own, the marriage remains a love match. With this inauspicious beginning marked by cross purposes, the young couple embark on married life.

"Fighting broke out again. David went out and fought the Philistines. He inflicted a great defeat upon them and they fled before him. Then [once again] an evil spirit of the Lord came upon Saul while he was sitting in his house with a spear in his hand, and David was playing (the lyre). Saul tried to pin David to the wall with the spear, but he eluded Saul, so that he drove the spear into the wall. David fled and got away."

The warrior-musician flees to his home, unaware that Saul

"sent messengers unto David's house to watch him and to slay him in the morning." Michal, however, anticipates her father's move. Having grown up in Saul's household, she knows too well the force of his rage and his irrational dark moods. She demonstrates her love for David by choosing to betray her father to save her husband.

Michal warns David, "Unless you run for your life tonight, you will be killed tomorrow." She lets David down from their window, and he escapes Saul's assassins. David utters not a word to express his feelings for Michal, although his speech to Goliath reveals a man whose well-chosen words can provoke a giant and inspire a nation. The Bible records no tearful farewell, no thanks, no promise that he will return for her. We certainly do not hear of a passionate embrace or kisses that "are sweeter than wine." He is more concerned with his own survival than with Michal's safety.

Hoping to mislead any pursuers, "Michal then took the household idol, laid it on the bed, and covered it with a cloth; and at its head she put a net of goat's hair. Saul sent messengers to seize David; but she said, 'He is sick.' Saul, however, sent back the messengers to see David for themselves. 'Bring him up to me in the bed,' he ordered, 'that he may be put to death.' When the messengers came, they found the household idol in the bed, with the net of goat's hair at its head."

Saul, furious, questions Michal, "Why did you play that trick on me and let my enemy get away safely?" Cornered, Michal lies that David had threatened her, "Help me get away or I'll kill you."

In urging David to escape, Michal acts quickly and decisively, though she must be troubled by the discord threatening to destroy her relationship with both her husband and her father. David trusts her as she lowers him through the window. Michal is left behind with the father she has betrayed while she waits for the husband she adores.

David's farewell to Michal is so cold and unappreciative that Michal loses confidence both in David's love for her and in herself. She does not join him as Sarah joined Abraham when he decided to leave Haran for a destination unknown. At this moment early in their marriage, she misses the opportunity to start forging a lifelong bond and be part of David's life for better or worse. For the moment, that life appears none too promising. After leaving her, David gathers around him hundreds of followers, desperate men who form an irregular army and hide in deserts and mountains, moving from place to place to escape Saul's spies and soldiers. But marriage is about sharing and building intimacy through living together and forging a joint history. Michal would have been better off staying involved in David's life, even if that meant exchanging the luxury of life in the royal court for physical hardship.

For Michal the decision is made more difficult because her father views David as a mortal threat to his reign. She must choose between her marriage and her obedience to her father the king. She cannot have both. David's place in their bed is now occupied by an inert household idol. The net of goat hair peeking from under the coverlet is a poor substitute for a live, red-blooded David. Her subterfuge brings to mind Rachel's theft of Laban's household gods. In both cases, a daughter—the younger of two sisters—rebels against a father's arbitrary rule. Both fathers are flummoxed by a graven image, and the joke is on them.

Once a rebel who helps her husband survive, Michal quickly becomes a pawn whose fate is determined by her father and her husband. To her father, Michal was a snare to entrap David; to David, she is a political convenience.

SAUL IS DETERMINED TO ELIMINATE any possible claim to the throne from David, based on his relationship to the royal family. Thus he seeks another political match for Michal, this time with a member of the tribe of Benjamin, Saul's own kin. The king seeks revenge not only against David but also against his rebellious daughter.

Saul arbitrarily pulls Michal out of her home, where she awaits David's return, and hands her over to Paltiel, son of Laish from Gallim. She is overwhelmed by the intensity of her father's wrath and her husband's ambition. King Saul's absolute authority over Michal recalls Laban's absolute authority over his two daughters, Rachel and Leah.

Paltiel is a footnote in biblical history, someone whose path briefly intersects with that of the royal family. We hear nothing about Michal's thoughts or her feelings about her new husband. We wonder if Michal found tranquillity with Paltiel, far from the machinations and intrigues of the court.

In his fury Saul violates a biblical law that forbids a woman not properly divorced from marrying another man; if there is a divorce, the original husband must participate in the proceedings. Saul, however, could have argued that David abandoned Michal and that according to the ancient Code of Hammurabi, if a husband disappears for a lengthy period, his wife can remarry and then go back to her first husband when and if he returns.

Michal's humiliation is compounded when word reaches her

that David has acquired two new wives, Achinoam of Jezreel and the widow Abigail. Though legal—even routine—in a polygamous society, David's actions must have seemed a betrayal to the princess, the woman who saved his life.

Meanwhile the war between Israel and the Philistines flares up again. "The Philistines attacked Israel, and many fell on Mount Gilboa." Saul and his three sons, including David's devoted friend Jonathan—Michal's brother—are among the fallen. "David . . . and all the men with him . . . lamented and wept, and they fasted until evening for Saul and his son Jonathan, and for the soldiers of the Lord and the House of Israel who had fallen by the sword."

David, the poet and the musician, intones a dirge over Saul and his son Jonathan:

> *Your glory, O Israel,*
> *Lies slain on your heights;*
> *How have the mighty fallen! . . .*
> *Saul and Jonathan,*
> *Beloved and cherished,*
> *Never parted*
> *In life or in death.*
> *They were swifter than eagles,*
> *They were stronger than lions!*
> *How have the mighty fallen,*
> *The weapons of war perished!*

MICHAL RECEDES FROM THE STORY for many chapters, as David spends years moving from desert to mountain caves to Philistine cities to escape Saul's men. When she finally reappears, it is because politics intrudes once again into her life. David, now anointed as king, demands that she be returned to him. She is no longer the young risk-taker who once challenged her father, now dead. Life has taken its toll. When she is taken from Paltiel, "her husband walked with her as far as Bahurim, weeping as he followed her; then Abner [commander of David's army] ordered him to turn back, and he went back."

When we meet Paltiel for the first and only time, he is a beaten, pathetic man forced to surrender his wife so that David can fortify his throne. Michal's reactions are obscured from us. Does she care for Paltiel? The Bible says nothing. But it appears that Paltiel loves Michal and is powerless to keep her.

No longer the innocent young bride, Michal has been returned to David. Theirs is a political marriage based on exclusively pragmatic terms. She once again suffers a devastating loss of self-respect and grows bitter and resentful.

David now has six other wives and numerous concubines. Michal must surrender any dream of a happy, fruitful life with David and confront the painful truth: her husband can—and does—choose to spend nights in beds other than hers. Michal and David are as emotionally detached from each other as they were physically distant during the years of their separation. Each wife except Michal bears David at least one son. Michal, however, remains childless and thus unable to consolidate her status in court as the first wife.

David "captured the stronghold of Zion . . . and renamed it the City of David. . . . David took more concubines and wives in Jerusalem, and more sons and daughters were born to David." He chooses Jerusalem as his capital because it is a neutral site not associated with any of the tribes of Israel. He also repossesses from the Philistines the Ark of the Lord, which symbolizes God's presence to the Israelites. The Ark is the wooden chest containing the two tablets of Moses inscribed with the Ten Commandments that the Hebrews carried with them to Canaan from Mount Sinai during the Exodus from Egypt. The Philistines overlaid it with gold but found it nonetheless brought them much tribulation. Now that David is established in the City of David, he assembles thirty thousand men to bring to his city the recovered Ark. He hopes that its presence will signal divine approval to the people of his choice of Jerusalem as the capital of his new kingdom.

David, a consummate political animal, celebrates his triumph in extravagant fashion. "David whirled with all his might before the Lord; David was girt with a linen ephod," the Bible notes, making it clear that David was barely clad. "Thus David and all the House of Israel brought up the Ark of the Lord with shouts and with blasts of the horn."

Michal is the one person who disapproves of the triumphant procession, a huge, exuberant crowd headed by her husband. She watches the celebration from afar, from David's palace. "As the Ark of the Lord entered the City of David, Michal daughter of Saul looked out of the window and saw King David leaping and whirling before the Lord; and she despised him for it."

The chronicler gives a detailed account of this dramatic moment in Israelite history: "They brought in the Ark of the Lord and set it up in its place inside the tent which David had pitched for it, and David sacrificed burnt offerings and offerings of well-being before the Lord. When David finished sacrificing the burnt offerings and the thank offerings, he blessed the people in the name of the Lord of Hosts. And he distributed among all the people—the entire multitude of Israel, man and woman alike—to each a loaf of bread, a cake made in a pan, and a raisin cake. Then all the people left for their homes."

King Saul's daughter proceeds to make one final, irretrievable mistake. Losing all self-control, she allows her repressed feelings of disappointment, hurt, disgust, and jealousy to rise to the surface. After the triumphant festivities, "David went home to greet his household. And Michal daughter of Saul came out to meet David and said, 'Didn't the king of Israel do himself honor today—exposing himself today in the sight of the slavegirls of his subjects, as one of the riffraff might expose himself!' "

David answers harshly, "It was before the Lord who chose me instead of your father and all his family and appointed me ruler over the Lord's people Israel! I will dance before the Lord and dishonor myself even more, and be low in my own esteem; but among the slavegirls that you speak of I will be honored."

The bitter episode concludes with a sentence that signals her utter isolation and misery, while delicately referring to the cessation of sexual relations between Michal and David: "So to her dying day Michal daughter of Saul had no children."

IN MICHAL'S EYES, HER HUSBAND the king conducts himself like a coarse commoner. His skimpy linen garment conceals little as he dances, and the women swoon. Michal finds this behavior a shockingly public display of his humble origins. She remembers that at the beginning of their marriage—as a devoted, enterprising wife—she helped David escape the assassins down a rope "through the window." This time, however, she has become a pitiable, enraged spectator gazing at her husband—and the Bible repeats the phrase—"through the window" and "from a distance."

The class difference between Michal and David widens into an unbridgeable chasm. The husband who has never loved her, who has never treated her with the respect due a princess, thrives among the common people, engaged in the religious rite of bringing the Ark of the Lord to Jerusalem. To Michal, the event is a circus, and her spouse is a caricature of a king. He distributes gifts of food among all the people, man and woman alike.

Michal's final downfall follows her public confrontation with David upon his return home, flinging the kinds of insults from which few marriages can recover. Her acerbic words eliminate any hope that her marriage might improve. From then on, Michal is David's wife in name only; her bed and womb remain empty. As Michal's moment in history nears its end, David behaves badly, flaunting his power and having the last word. But Michal is the first to cross the line that exists in every marriage: she humiliates her husband in public. As the biblical writers understand so well, words are a gift that you can employ to wound or to heal, and they must be used with utmost care.

Where did this couple go wrong, and what lesson emerges from the torturous course of their marriage? They start out on an unequal footing. She falls in love with a hero who only a short while back was an earthy, scrappy shepherd. A princess, she is accustomed to being obeyed and admired. Emotionally too they are worlds apart. She is in love and eager for companionship. David, preoccupied with climbing the ladder of fame and defending the kingdom's borders, is rarely available to her emotionally or physically. Even in the beginning, he is not attracted to her personally but only desires her as a political stepping-stone. When she discovers her father plotting to murder her husband, she boldly allies herself with her husband, showing resourcefulness in arranging his escape and deceiving the assassins. For years to follow, however, she has no more contact with him. From that time on she loses her self-confidence and finds herself at the mercy of her father's emotional swings and her husband's soaring ambitions. Years later she takes her place as a king's wife, but by then she is unable to adjust to the changed circumstances. Her husband has become a greater celebrity than she is.

We all know intimate details of high-profile marriages throughout history in which a spouse tolerates episodes of infidelity in exchange for status, wealth, or access to power. Such couples seem to reach an understanding, an arrangement, suppressing pain, humiliation, and frustration, and their marriages often endure long after most men and women would call it quits. Unlike Rebecca, who becomes frustrated with Isaac yet stays the course, Michal refuses to take a realistic view of the spouse she fell in love with or the options available to her. Michal could not have cured her wounded feelings, but she would have been wise to take account of the social strictures of her day and keep them under her control. Without that realistic attitude, any marriage is doomed.

Michal's tragedy is that she falls in love with a talented man of many parts—warrior, poet, musician, statesman, and canny politician—who is handsome and charming. Moreover, as the Bible reminds us and David firmly believes, God is with him. But Michal does not have the wisdom or maturity to handle the ambitious, charismatic husband she hardly knows, and she ends up despising him for the very qualities that attracted her in the first place. In their final scene together he is the same national hero she met years before, but she cannot appreciate his strengths and focuses only on his limitations.

Most biblical heroines, with the exception of Sarah, who rescues Abraham by joining Pharaoh's harem, do not literally save their husbands' lives. But they all support their men and are indispensable to them in their commitments to build a family, a tribe, or a nation. Unlike the matriarchs, Michal has not been part of her husband's tumultuous life and is now jealous of his accomplishments. As a young bride she should have followed David into the desert and shared his risks and achievements, but as a king's daughter she was not prepared to take on the rough life of an outlaw. Perhaps Michal, passionate about David, assumed he would send for her. As a king's daughter she may have felt she was someone very special who would never be ignored or shunted aside. Her youth, her upbringing, and her pride may have prevented her from realizing that to David she was no more than a useful political tool.

Other biblical women are as outspoken as Michal. Neither Sarah nor Rachel hold back their anger and frustration, but they give vent to their feelings privately. In the biblical chronicle, Abigail, Bathsheba, the widow Tamar, and Queen Esther excel in showing tact and choosing the right words and occasion to steer their partners in the right direction. But these women are all confident that they are loved and respected by their partners. There is no evidence that Michal is loved by her father, and in any event, he is erratic at best; as for David, he is her first and only love, but he is unresponsive to her. In today's language, she is emotionally deprived. Some have even speculated that David resents Saul's daughter from the very beginning because their different social backgrounds seem to be a source of irritation and hostility. He may have taken advantage of her outburst in Jerusalem to banish her from his life.

The evenhandedness of the biblical text allows readers to identify with the rage of either protagonist. Michal's explosion is understandable and even justified, erupting after years of neglect, but she does not understand that how and when we say something is as important as what we say. (Millennia after Michal, we are still making these mistakes on a daily basis.) She chooses the worst possible moment to denigrate him—in public and at the triumphal celebration when David is finally bringing the Ark into his city.

David's response to Michal is cruel and petty. In recoil, he stoops to her level by returning the most brutally hurtful observations he can think of. As the man with all the power and glory, he should have shown magnanimity to this woman who has no power and whom he has abandoned for so many years.

Emotionally, Michal needs David more than he needs her. Despite this disadvantaged position, she never learns to accept that David is who he is and is not about to change. David may offer status and comfort, and he might father a child. But she is foolish to count on him to be an attentive husband. In a polygamous society, he is faithful to no one.

Michal is conspicuously absent in the pivotal moments of David's rise to power as well as his fall from grace. She does not accompany him during the difficult early years when he hides from her father's wrath. Nor is she with him when he becomes an even greater hero to the nation by accompanying the Ark up to

Jerusalem. He is at one with his people, and they love him. She stays aloof from both his wars and his triumph.

David and Michal are locked into the Bible's most unhappy marriage, and the biblical narrator does not shrink from exposing the raw edges of their private life. The lesson is as valid for contemporary relationships as it was three thousand years ago; when it comes to marriage, we must not take a spouse's feelings for granted, however just we may feel our cause to be. David is the king and has all the power in the relationship; she has none. Michal would be more likely to get what she wanted if she tried to do what worked rather than remaining a prisoner of her notions about the way things ought to be.

An important predictor of modern-day divorce is not whether you argue with your spouse but rather *how* you argue, and how the argument comes to an end. One of the first things to go in a marriage is civility. Verbal abuse, name-calling (also known as verbal sadism), and character assassination are demeaning and humiliating; they destroy self-esteem and human dignity. They destroy the chance of any further communication. Civility and manners are a behavioral manifestation of self-restraint. Often considered by the young as "phony," they are a way of taming one's immediate gut response. They give us the space to consider how acting out through inappropriate behavior will affect others. Self-restraint also entails being alert to other people's facial expressions, their particular character, their sensitivities—paying attention to who they really are. We need to remember to think before we talk. Self-restraint and sensitivity are a form of respect. Love cannot be legislated, but respect must be expected and demanded. It is the indispensable prerequisite for harmony, absent which the couple will grow distant and hostile. If children are present, they will mimic disrespectful behavior, and sadly, it will mark their adult lives.

These lessons are as valid for contemporary couples as they were three thousand years ago. As the saying goes, couples must grow together or they will grow apart. As Michal's story points out, ideally they should fall and rise together.

EIGHT

ABIGAIL:

DAVID MEETS HIS MATCH

W HEN THE FAIR ABIGAIL MEETS David, the onetime protégé of Israel's first king, Saul, he is a fugitive on the run. He survives as an outlaw in the wilderness of Paran, shielded from the king's army by his admirers, some six hundred men as rugged as their mountain refuge. They live by their wits, unsure of their next meal. The people of Israel love the ruddy hero who slew Goliath and fought the Philistines on their behalf. Some want him to be their king. A rumor is abroad in the land that God has already chosen David to take the throne from Saul. The Bible observes, "Saul was afraid of David because the Lord was with him but had departed from Saul."

The biblical narrator introduces the couple who will test the mettle of the plucky upstart David: "There was a man in Maon whose possessions were in Carmel. The man was very wealthy; he owned three thousand sheep and a thousand goats. At the time, he was shearing his sheep in Carmel. The man's name was Nabal, and his wife's name was Abigail. The woman was intelligent and beautiful, but the man, a Calebite, was a hard man and an evildoer."

One way David and his fellow fugitives support themselves is by offering armed protection to nearby landowners. During the festive sheepshearing season, David sends ten men to call on Nabal to deliver a message couched in elaborately courteous words. He instructs his emissary to greet Nabal in the name of David, the son of Jesse, ask how he fares, voice satisfaction that he is faring well, and express the wish that next year at the same time both he and his house fare equally well. Then they are to remind Nabal that "your shepherds have been with us; we did not harm them and nothing of theirs was missing all the time they were in Carmel. Ask your young men and they will tell you." Finally they will reveal the purpose of the mission: "Please give your servants and your son David whatever you can."

David's strength in numbers gives him certain strategic advantages vis-à-vis individual landowners, but he also feels entitled to the food he and his men desperately need. Taken aback by the brash demand, Nabal mocks the messenger's leader: "Who is David? Who is the son of Jesse? There are many slaves nowadays who run away from their masters. Should I then take my bread and my water and the meat that I slaughtered for my own shearers, and give them to men who come from I don't know where?"

Nabal sends David's men away without a morsel from his

abundant stores. When his men report Nabal's response, David's temper flares. He vows that by morning not one of Nabal's men will be alive; he and four hundred of his warriors will teach Nabal and his household a lesson.

Nabal's men understand that their master's ill-considered reply has doomed them. They have lived among David's men, whom they describe as making up "a wall about us both by night and by day all the time we were with them tending the flocks." They know the consequences of angering a hotheaded youth in trouble with the law. They turn to Nabal's wife, Abigail, and here we get our first glimpse of Abigail's character and the respect she inspires. Nabal's men trust her to deal wisely and constructively with both David and Nabal.

Abigail listens as she is asked to "consider carefully what you should do, for harm threatens our master and all his household." Heedless of a hired hand's customary servility, the young go-between bursts out that Nabal is "such a nasty fellow that no one can speak to him."

Abigail does not procrastinate. Like Tamar's resolve in disguising herself as a harlot and Rebecca prodding Jacob to receive his father's blessing, Abigail responds decisively, using all her wits. Quickly she gathers together a huge quantity of food: two hundred loaves of bread, two jugs of wine, parched corn, a hundred raisin cakes, and two hundred fig cakes, as well as five sheep readied for eating. She loads the donkeys and heads for the mountains where David and his men are hiding out. She says not a word to her husband, however, about what she plans to do.

Thus begins one of the Bible's most daunting diplomatic missions.

Abigail meets David as he and his men, girded for battle, are "hurtling down a trail on a hillside." David, venting his anger, is swearing as he leads his band toward Nabal's homestead: "All in vain did I guard everything that belonged to this fellow in the wilderness, and nothing was missing from all that was his, and he paid me back evil for good!" David calls upon the Almighty to finish off this ingrate if he fails to wreak revenge, using a vulgarity to denote the men of Nabal's household: "May God do thus and more to the enemies of David, if, by the light of morning, I leave a single one who pees against a wall." (This is a direct translation from the Hebrew.)

Facing an angry mob of sword-wielding young men roused for vengeance, Abigail remains calm and confident. Her words betray no fear. She treats David as if he were royalty, even though his actions toward her husband smack of banditry.

In accord with the etiquette of the day, Abigail dismounts from her donkey upon seeing David approach, then throws herself at his feet, flinging her face to the ground as a sign of her complete submission to his will and whim. In her opening sentence she startles David by calling herself his "handmaid" and describing herself as responsible for the misunderstanding with her husband: "Mine, my lord, is the blame."

Abigail knows David is hostile and angry. Rather than accuse him of violent behavior, which he might well have expected, she takes the responsibility for the "problem" on her shoulders, thereby defusing the tension. Her behavior highlights most women's preference for resolving conflict through persuasion rather than physical violence, knowing that cooperation is preferable to brute force.

Because Abigail speaks as a humble supplicant of lower rank

rather than angrily, as might be expected, she lessens David's need to be defensive. At the same time she conveys sympathy for the situation he finds himself in. She then shrewdly and subtly shifts the blame to Nabal by pointing out that she did not meet with David's messengers. She further distances herself from her husband by dismissing him contemptuously, calling on David to "pay no attention to that wretched fellow Nabal." Her summation is devastating: "For he is just what his name says. His name (in Hebrew) means 'boor' and he is a boor." At this point she has disarmed David even more.

Abigail's next rhetorical foray compares David to the Lord, and she launches her principal argument, which is simple: David must not stain his hand with blood. With stylistic virtuosity, she plays with words, linking David, whom she calls her "lord," and the Lord Who is in Heaven: "As the Lord lives and as you live—the Lord who has kept you from seeking redress by blood with your own hands—let your enemies and all who would harm my lord fare like Nabal! . . . For the Lord will grant my lord an enduring house because my lord is fighting the battles of the Lord and no wrong is ever to be found in you. . . . And when the Lord has accomplished for my lord all the good He has promised you and has appointed you ruler of Israel, do not let this be a cause of stumbling and of faltering courage to my lord that you have shed blood needlessly and that my lord sought redress with his own hands."

With this framing of David's conflict with Nabal, Abigail ties David's fortunes to God's protection and generosity. She interlaces her references to "the Lord" (the Divine) and "my lord" (the mortal David) so repeatedly and audaciously that she may well coax a knowing smile from the warrior who is also a poet. Although David's sword is still poised to kill her husband and the men of their household, Abigail nevertheless credits God for preventing David "from seeking redress by blood with your own hands." Within moments she has promoted this bold statement to the level of prophecy, projecting David as God's choice for Israel's next king.

Elevating a turf dispute between a fugitive outlaw and a rich landowner, she suggests that David is "fighting the battles of the Lord" and thus will vanquish all his enemies just as surely as he will vanquish Nabal. She predicts that no evil will be found in David in all his days and that the dynasty he establishes will be enduring. Vividly—and correctly—she conjures up the near future and invents a cunning metaphor that encompasses David's triumph over Goliath by means of a slingshot: "If men rise up to pursue you and to seek your life, the life of my lord shall be bound in the bundle of the living in the care of the Lord your God; and the lives of your enemies He shall sling out as from the hollow of a sling." Her conclusion bridges theology and logic, moral righteousness and political expediency: "And when the Lord has accomplished for my lord all the good that He has promised you, and has appointed you ruler over Israel, do not let this be a cause of stumbling and of faltering courage to my lord that you have shed blood needlessly and that my lord sought redress with his own hands."

In the midst of submitting to David these conjoined theses, Abigail deftly draws attention to their shared heritage and faith. Her repeated references to God—*Adonai* in the Hebrew text—make it clear that she is not talking about some idol of the neighboring tribes but about the one and only God, the God of Israel whose commandment forbids murder. She knows that David understands what she means when cautioning against bloodguilt and the consequent spiral of revenge. She suggests the kind of intimacy that exists between two like-minded people, inviting David to turn her petition into a dialogue between two Israelites with the same moral code of behavior. With subtlety, tact, and confidence, she uses every tool in her arsenal: persuasion, political advice, religious ethics, and flattery.

At the end of her lengthy plea Abigail coolly appends a brief request for a general personal favor, as if it were a mere after-thought: "And when the Lord has prospered my lord, remember your maid." She is smart enough to know that any contact with a powerful or potentially powerful personage should be capitalized on. David takes note of the oblique invitation but, functioning as a prudent leader, makes no commitment and offers no comment. In an earlier but similarly parenthetical remark—but no doubt the most enticing to the band of hungry men surrounding them—she refers to the ample provisions she has brought along, variously translated as "the blessing" or "the present" for "the young men who go about in the footsteps of my lord."

Within the space of a few sentences, Abigail progresses from acknowledging all iniquity to pleading for mercy to referring to much-needed provisions to offering political advice to the fugitive whom she announces will be the next king to requesting future po-litical favor.

Abigail's plea to David is the Hebrew Bible's longest single quotation attributed to a woman. A masterpiece of meticulously crafted phrases, her argument relies on the art of flattery, one of the oldest tools of civilized discourse. Her speech offers David time to reconsider his wish for revenge born of a flash of fury. He also may fear that ignoring Nabal's refusal to feed his men would be viewed as cowardly. By the time Abigail finishes, he is won over.

David abandons the idea of a bloodbath. Her diplomacy and the quantities of food she brings with her divert David from the political and moral error of revenge that might have stained his future reign and perhaps even prevented it.

David's reply honors Abigail by echoing her extravagant references to the Lord and His elect, David: "Praised be the Lord, the God of Israel who sent you this day to meet me! And blessed be your prudence and blessed be you for restraining me from seeking redress in blood by my own hands." David's language, referring to the sixth commandment, against murder, is couched in the religious terms of Israel, familiar to Abigail. His wording further confirms that he and Abigail are accountable to the same God.

Nevertheless, David is not so pious as to resist the temptation of repeating his threat to kill Nabal and his men, and he exaggerates the danger that faces Abigail as well. He grumbles, "For as sure as the Lord, the God of Israel lives—who has kept me from harming you—had you not come quickly to meet me, not a single male of Nabal's line would have been left by daybreak."

David makes sure that Abigail knows her words have swayed him. "See, I have heeded your plea and respected your wish." He proves himself big enough to acknowledge that he, the renowned warrior, owes something to a seemingly powerless woman groveling at his feet. The concession is all the more striking for having occurred in a "macho" culture in which an acknowledgment of help from a woman could be seen as weakness. She has taught him a lesson he will never forget—to consider before he acts on gut responses of revenge. He bids her farewell: "Go up in peace to your house."

The text reveals no overt sexual attraction between Abigail

and David. But between the lines of their very formal exchange, the reader can sense romantic undertones in her generous, flattering words, her solicitousness, and the air of secrecy surrounding their meeting. David, marooned in the wilderness with a bunch of uncouth men, could hardly have failed to notice that Abigail is a desirable woman "of good understanding, and of a beautiful countenance."

One reason for David's self-restraint may be that he is young, in his early twenties if not younger, while Abigail is older, or at least she sounds older and far more mature.

Abigail leaves David with no suggestion of another meeting or a possible future relationship. This ends the secret encounter with David and we hear of no more.

But the biblical narrator is ready to please the reader by adding one more twist.

After handing over to David the provisions she brought, Abigail returns home, where she finds Nabal drunk in the midst of his sheepshearing feast. She decides to wait until morning to tell him about her mission to David. When Nabal hears what she has done, he suffers what is probably either a stroke or a heart attack. The text, terse and dispassionate, says that "his heart died within him and he became as a stone. And about ten days later the Lord smote Nabal; and he died."

What exactly did Abigail tell her husband and what did she omit? Which aspect of her encounter with David caused Nabal's heart to turn into stone? The Bible relies on the reader to fill in the gaps with his own imagination and experience.

When David learns that Nabal is dead, he credits God with eliminating his foe. He says, "Praised be the Lord who championed my cause against the insults of Nabal and held back His servant from wrongdoing; the Lord has brought Nabal's wrongdoing down on his own head."

Next David sends messengers to propose marriage to Abigail. She "immediately bowed low with her face to the ground and said, 'Your handmaid is ready to be your maidservant, to wash the feet of my lord's servants.'" Then Abigail "rose quickly and mounted a donkey." With five of her handmaids in attendance, she follows David's messengers and becomes his wife. Yet again Abigail causes events to move forward quickly, and once again the narrator makes note of her actions.

For the widow Abigail, Nabal's death is well timed, as is David's prompt decision to send for her. Once again Abigail wastes not a moment in seizing her opportunity; she happily hurries after David. Undoubtedly relieved to be free from her marriage to Nabal, Abigail links her fate to David's.

The Bible records that Abigail joins David when he leaves the wilderness of Paran to escape Saul and flees to the Philistine city of Gath to seek protection. When the Amalekites, Israel's mortal enemies, invade from the south, they take Abigail prisoner, but David's men strike back and rescue her. After Saul's death David and Abigail move to Hebron, where David is anointed King of Judea and Abigail bears him a son, Chileab.

IN CONFRONTING AN ANGRY YOUNG outlaw with her petition, Abigail takes her life and the lives of those in her household in her hands. She is a defenseless woman whose world is on the verge of collapse, but with great tact and rhetorical skill, she challenges a warlord to refrain from violence. She threads her way between two stubborn, hardheaded men locking horns—her husband and David. Her main tool for survival is the gift of language that God first gave to Adam in the Garden of Eden, and she wields it brilliantly as she pleads, flatters, reasons, and persuades.

Her flattery of David, while a successful tactic of self-preservation, also averts actions that would be both morally objectionable and impolitic for David. What alternatives are available to Abigail other than this high-risk course? Unlike contemporary women, she cannot separate herself from her husband or move to another town. If she does not deal directly with David, her husband will perish with his men, leaving her in a perilous position and, as her husband's wife and thus a leader in society, morally complicit in the death of their followers. She defuses the conflict with feminine tact and demonstrates that brute masculine force is not the only solution to hostile confrontation between individuals or groups.

In responding to Abigail, David displays intelligence and intuition. Just as Abigail appeals to David's ambition and ego, he perceives her strengths. Like the best of politicians, he praises her unique qualities and avoids platitudes, which she would, in any event, discount. He does not allude to her beauty but lauds her wisdom and decisive action. By the end of his encounter with Abigail, David has come one step closer to behaving like a true and worthy king. He controls his murderous impulses and thereby passes a test of leadership.

David's greatness lies in his capacity to articulate his appreciation of this woman's courage and initiative. Abigail and David are cut from the same cloth: both are survivors. Gallantly and with political savvy, he tells her, "See, I have heeded your plea and respected your wish." He could easily have ignored or forgotten her request to "remember your maid," but instead he provides her refuge when Nabal dies. (Her unhappy marriage might well have been another of Abigail's hidden motives in her decision to approach David.) By marrying Abigail, David protects the widow, in those days as vulnerable as a child or a foreigner.

Unhappily, the Bible makes no further mention of Abigail. I like to think that as they age, David continues to consult her as his adviser, even his confidante. But the biblical narrator focuses only on Abigail's profound impact on David's conduct years before he becomes king.

Abigail's role in the bloodstained drama of David's rise to power is more than a cameo appearance. The chapter in 1 Samuel that revolves around Abigail is inserted in a book chronicling the battles of the failed king Saul and his victorious successor David. It is at least partly due to Abigail's power of persuasion that David the young warrior evolves into David the king, who is raised above all his nation's other kings, beloved through generations by his people, for whom he can do no wrong.

The young David is the man to fall in love with. He is the heroic warrior, bold and crafty, a natural leader, "ruddy with fine eyes." He makes no pretense at romance, promising nothing to his women. His is a polygamous world, and he exploits it fully. When he beckons, women respond.

GIVEN THE SENSITIVITY OF THE text detailing Abigail's actions and words, it strikes me that 1 Samuel 25 might very well have been written by a woman. A female author would certainly have been an exception among those writing the Hebrew Bible, but then, Abigail is an exception among women. She is confident, intuitive, capable, resourceful, persuasive, and very brave. She embodies the feminine proclivity to resolve conflict through words rather than violence. Using her feminine sensibilities to best advantage, she is not afraid to say "remember me" to the powerful. She does not consider being female a liability.

NINE

BATHSHEBA AND DAVID:
FROM LUST TO LOVE

THREE THOUSAND YEARS AGO DAVID was at the zenith of his power. He had united the northern and the southern tribes of his people into one kingdom, and he had declared Jerusalem its spiritual and political capital in perpetuity. David the public man is at peace, but the private man is restless. One lazy afternoon he sees a married woman and covets her. While the narrative simmers with anger at the abuse of royal power, it also traces how a moment of fleeting lust grows into an enduring partnership.

The youngest of seven brothers, David has worked his way up from being a shepherd to becoming a confident, even complacent monarch accustomed to being obeyed and having his wishes granted. Most of his marriages are arranged to strengthen political alliances and to breed heirs to the throne. Concubines are available to choose from in response to any whim. Nothing in his married life hints at love.

One spring the veteran warrior decides for the very first time not to join his soldiers as they go off to battle. He takes siestas, he is moody, perhaps going through what we now call a midlife crisis. He wanders aimlessly through the royal palace. He is unaccustomed to so much idle time.

"At the turn of the year, the season when kings go out [to battle], . . . David remained in Jerusalem" while "his officers" and "all Israel" were risking their lives. The story begins at a leisurely pace. "Late one afternoon, David rose from his couch and strolled on the roof of the royal palace; and from the roof he saw a woman bathing. The woman was very beautiful, and the king sent someone to make inquiries about her. He reported, 'She is Bathsheba, daughter of Eliam and wife of Uriah, the Hittite.'"

Archaeologists suggest that from the elevation of the royal dwelling on a hillside, David enjoyed a panoramic view of the houses below. After one glance at the naked Bathsheba, David is smitten. He lusts, he covets, and he takes action.

In an arrogant display of power, he sends emissaries to fetch Bathsheba. With her husband, a professional soldier, off fighting, she responds to David's call and "lies with him—she had just purified herself after her period—and she went back home. The woman conceived and she sent word to David, 'I am pregnant.'"

There is no hint of coercion, but some suggest that Bathsheba had no choice but to accede to David's invitation. Can a commoner refuse a king? At that time monarchs had absolute power and were not held accountable for their private lives. Many in power even today—politicians, athletes, movie stars—abuse their power and take liberties with lesser mortals. Women in the Western world have more options, including legal action, which were not available to women in Bathsheba's times. On the other hand, why was she bathing on the low-lying roof of a house in a city built on hills? Did she expect privacy? What was she thinking about?

The spare biblical account of the sexual liaison between David and Bathsheba is clearly not intended to titillate the reader. Bathsheba's feelings go unrecorded. Rather, the narrative focuses on the perennial impulse of lust to illustrate deeper lessons about the consequences of abusing one's power, even as other parts of the narrative praise David's many extraordinary virtues as a musician, a poet, and the author of hundreds of psalms, including the beloved Twenty-third Psalm, "The Lord Is My Shepherd."

David is an exceptional man—nonetheless human and fallible.

Though David is infatuated with Bathsheba, he is not about to snatch a wife permanently away from her husband. Bathsheba's devastating note, however, the first recorded communication between the two, demands new thinking. The note consists of only three words, "I am pregnant," but its subtext is "What are you going to do about this?" The terse message offers a first glimpse into Bathsheba's forceful and defiant character. From this note David understands that Bathsheba will not simply vanish. She is no scullery maid, to be used and discarded. She will not be ignored or acquiesce to the role of a "woman scorned." She expects David, the man with the power, who is her lover and happens to be the king, to extricate her and her unborn child from her dangerous situation.

She has no alternative. Her tone is matter-of-fact. She does not grovel, beg, or flatter, even though she knows that the penalty for adultery at that time and place is stoning. If David does not intervene, she and their child will die a hideously painful and public death.

True to his nature, David takes immediate action to contain the damage; the pregnancy is becoming visible. He settles on a plan of cover-up to disguise the baby's royal paternity.

He tells Joab, his trusted chief of staff, " 'Send me Uriah the Hittite.' And Joab sent Uriah to David. When Uriah came to him, David asked him how Joab and the troops were faring and how the war was going. Then David said to Uriah, 'Go down to your house and bathe your feet.' When Uriah left the royal palace, a present from the king followed him."

David orders Uriah home for a conjugal visit and plies him with rich food and drink from the palace, hoping that the unborn child can be passed off as Bathsheba's husband's. Uriah, however, balks. Declining to accept better treatment than that available to his fellow soldiers, he refuses the king's offer. "Uriah slept at the entrance of the royal palace, along with the other officers of his lord, and did not go down to his house," the Bible notes. "When David was told that Uriah had not gone down to his house, he said to Uriah, 'You just came from a journey; why have you not gone down to your house?' Uriah answered David, 'The Ark and Israel and Judah are located at Succoth, and my master Joab and Your Majesty's men are camped in the open; how can I go home and eat and drink and sleep with my wife? As you live, by your very life, I will not do this thing!' " With his last sentence, Uriah alludes to David's having shirked his duty by not joining the battle with his men as he had always done previously.

David's actions are characteristic. Decisively and confidently, he tries to hide the results of his adultery, but, in an early example of the biblical roots of the rule of law, he is about to learn that even a king is not above the law. Once one starts down a morally slippery slope, even with a small misstep, the consequences are often uncontrollable. So it is for David as his strategy heads toward disaster.

The resourceful king tries one more time. He bids Uriah remain in Jerusalem another day. That night David dines with Uriah and they drink until Uriah gets drunk. But once again Uriah sleeps in camp with his soldiers and does not return to his home.

Bathsheba's husband is an enigmatic figure in this woeful tale. At first we admire his unwillingness to set himself apart from his men and his insistence on his honor as a soldier. After long abstinence he can resist the unexpected gift of a night with this wife whose allure is such that she has attracted the king's notice across the rooftops of Jerusalem. On the other hand, he may be cold or sexually unresponsive or so little in need of her that her company does not entice him. Or has word of his wife's affair reached him in the field? Does he wonder at the king's attentiveness to him in the midst of a military campaign? Is it his honor or is it anger at his wife that causes him to refuse to enter this triangle with the king? The biblical narrator provides no insight into Uriah's motives. His recorded words express only his stubborn lack of cooperation as he declines David's invitation—an unusually bold measure in light of the absolute, indeed sacred, authority of his king.

In the morning David commands Uriah to deliver a letter to Joab with orders for his chief of staff: "Place Uriah in the front line where the fighting is the fiercest; then fall back so that he may be killed." Uriah carries his own sealed death warrant to the battlefield. Joab obeys David's command and sends back the news that the king has been anxiously awaiting: "Your servant Uriah the Hittite was among those killed." David replies, giving Joab the spin he wants his general to put on Uriah's death: "Do not be distressed about the matter. The sword always takes its toll."

David shows no remorse for getting rid of Bathsheba's husband. If Uriah had remained alive to bear witness to the fruits of his wife's betrayal, Bathsheba would have been publicly stoned. The choice was between Bathsheba and Uriah. One of the two had to die, and David chose Uriah.

Although Bathsheba is integral to the story, her voice is absent. She carries the king's child, but we never learn how she is affected by knowing her husband is murdered because of her tryst with the king, or indeed if she knows this at all. But Jerusalem must have been rife with rumors that reached Bathsheba's ears. The people know that David cannot marry Bathsheba while her husband is alive. Once Uriah dies, her future is uncertain. "She lamented over her husband," the Bible says. "After the period of mourning was over, David sent and had her brought into his palace," where she becomes his wife. The child growing within her tightens the bond between the king and his new wife. The day she bathed on the low roof of her house now seems long ago, although only weeks have passed.

David resumes his daily life, thinking he has gotten away with his crime, but one foreboding line in the Bible warns that all is not well: "The thing that David had done was evil in the eyes of the Lord."

.   .   .

WITHOUT WARNING, DAVID IS VISITED by the prophet Nathan, like other biblical prophets a severe social critic whose messages are permeated with righteousness and passion. The prophets' motives have little to do with political schemes or personal ambitions. They are human beings through whom God speaks.

Nathan tells David a story. "There were two men in the same city, one rich and one poor. . . . One day a traveler came to the rich man, but he was loath to take anything from his own flocks or herds to prepare a meal for the guest who had come to him; so he took the poor man's lamb and prepared it for the man who had come to him."

At this tale of greed and theft, David flies into a rage and tells Nathan, "As the Lord lives, the man who did this deserves to die!"

Coolly Nathan points his finger at David and declares, "That man is you!" Then Nathan quotes the Lord, the God of Israel: "Why have you flouted the command of the Lord and done what displeases Him? You have put Uriah the Hittite to the sword; you took his wife and made her your wife and had him killed by the sword of the Ammonites. Therefore the sword shall never depart from your house. . . . I will make a calamity rise against you from within your own house."

The prophet's words shatter David's indifference and complacency. There is no merciful equivocation—only moral outrage. David breaks God's laws when he lies with Bathsheba, but it is his callous murder of Bathsheba's husband that provokes God's special wrath. The phrase with which David so dismissively accounted for Uriah's death, "The sword always takes its toll," now cuts the other way as God decrees, "The sword shall never depart from your house."

At last David faces the truth as the enormity of his wrongdoing begins to register with him, and he says to Nathan, "I stand guilty before the Lord!"

Nathan replies, "The Lord has remitted your sin; you shall not die." Forgiveness does not come fully or instantly. The first promised calamity comes soon: "The Lord afflicted the child that Uriah's wife had borne to David, and it became critically ill."

Begging God to spare his son, he fasts, prays, and sleeps on the ground at the child's side. But the infant dies.

David is powerless to alter God's decree. Racked with guilt and grief, he is convinced that his son has paid with his innocent life for his father's feckless lust and consequent murderous act. The king is well aware that had he not succumbed to temptation, the rest of the tragic tale would not have followed.

After the child dies, David springs back into action, to the puzzlement of his household. With a rapid succession of nine simple verbs, the Bible describes how "David rose from the ground; he bathed and anointed himself, and he changed his clothes. He went into the House of the Lord and prostrated himself. Then he went home and asked for food, which they set before him, and he ate. His courtiers asked him, 'Why have you acted in this manner? While the child was alive, you fasted and wept; but now that the child is dead, you rise and take food!' "

David replies, speaking for every parent who has lost a child, "Can I bring him back again? I shall go to him, but he will never come back to me."

David, a religious man, understands that his son's death does not atone for his sin and that his life will never be the same. In Psalm 51 he pleads for forgiveness:

Wash me thoroughly of my iniquity,
And purify me of my sin;
For I recognize my transgressions,
And am ever conscious of my sin.

David recognizes that he deserves divine punishment, which in turn helps him accept the pain he feels and return to his royal responsibilities. Thanks to his faith and his decisiveness, he apparently deals with the tragedy in a way that Bathsheba, the infant's mother, cannot.

"David consoled Bathsheba, his wife, and he came to her and lay with her, and she bore a son and called his name Solomon, and God loved him."

The king has murdered and the king has lied, but Bathsheba is still able to stir in him a tenderness we have not witnessed before. In her grief Bathsheba turns to David for consolation and leans on him for strength and understanding. Men are more likely to find solace and support in sexual intimacy, but David understands that a mother's needs are different. The biblical narrator makes a point of telling us that first David consoles Bathsheba and only then do they resume their sexual relationship.

David and Bathsheba move beyond simple lust, as every couple must if their partnership is to endure. They share their grief with an emotional intensity that David has not found with any of his other wives. Paradoxically, the death of their son ushers in a lifelong partnership that will mature and deepen through the years.

All too often the opposite occurs. Many marriages disintegrate after a child dies because husbands and wives grieve differently and deal with the pain in separate ways. They may find it difficult to meet each other's physical and emotional needs. One may need to express feelings at length while the other may need to repress them. One may blame the other for the tragedy, undermining their partnership with guilt and accusations.

Bathsheba bears another son, Solomon, and with the birth of the infant, the bond between Bathsheba and David deepens. But the power of divine punishment has not yet run its course. In the next generation, David's older children suffer one misfortune after another until the family history culminates in the tragedy of Absalom, who rebels against his father. When Absalom is killed, rather than being relieved that his son's insurrection has been put down, David is inconsolable. His powerful emotions reflect the feelings of almost all parents, who are devoted even in the face of truculence and rebellion. David "went up to the upper chamber . . . and wept, moaning these words as he went, 'My son Absalom! O my son, my son Absalom! If only I had died instead of you! O Absalom, my son, my son'!"

THE TIMELESS STORY OF BATHSHEBA and David's love affair echoes down the ages to our very day.

The story provokes questions about power, lust, deception, and guilt, and invites a diversity of observations that have since become almost universally accepted. The history of David warns us that power can transform and corrupt the individual. As Lord Acton famously put it, "Power tends to corrupt; absolute power corrupts absolutely." That alone, lust attracts but is limited to the first stage of a relationship and is later outgrown; that deception may seem useful in the short run but ultimately breeds distrust and can lead to larger misdeeds. David tries his best to cover up his adultery by pretending to be interested in Uriah's welfare, but the more he tries to persuade the husband to spend time with his wife, the more Uriah seems to distrust the king's motives and refuses to go along with David's scheme.

True guilt is a painful internal struggle with our conscience. It prompts us to be more sensitive to and aware of others. We feel guilty when we know we have failed to live up to our values and ideals and that we have hurt others. David feels genuine anguish when he realizes that he is like the rich man who took the only lamb belonging to the poor man. The guilty king feels that the loss of his infant son was a deserved punishment for his crime.

The issues of temptation and coveting that confront David and Bathsheba are as relevant to us today as they were then. The fateful journey that culminated in murder started with one small step before David even spotted Bathsheba bathing. Once he shirked his duty and stayed home instead of leading his troops in battle, he had begun on a downward path that led ultimately to murder. His unlimited royal power amplified by eager yes-men produced a sense of boundless entitlement. All these factors came together on a lazy afternoon on which the ethical standards of his faith seemed rather remote.

David does not blame "that woman" Bathsheba for "leading him astray" but assumes full responsibility for his conduct. In this he is unlike Adam, who blames Eve for his having disobeyed God in the Garden of Eden. It may be that David's acceptance of his guilt and responsibility for what happened is the very reason that God forgives David and allows him to stay on the throne.

The story of David and Bathsheba is a prime example of the Bible's "tough love" approach to life. The Bible acknowledges that humans are both vulnerable and fallible, but it also holds us responsible for our actions. It teaches us that sexual behavior must be subordinate to a tradition of moral and ethical beliefs, and that lying to cover up sexual or other misdeeds is wrong. When David flouts this rule of life, the consequences of his behavior impinge on the lives of his children and bring misery and loss into his private life. The death of a child is the worst tragedy in a parent's life and the harshest possible punishment.

The Ten Commandments constitute an ethical and spiritual code handed down to the Israelites as a basic daily guide by a concerned and loving God. In biblical times violating the seventh commandment on adultery would lead to stoning. Today we may choose marital counseling and divorce. "Thou shall not commit adultery" forewarns us that adultery destroys the bonds of trust that hold a couple together and threatens the stability of three generations—the couple, their children, and their grandparents. But despite the clarity of the Ten Commandments, human beings respond to myriad temptations in their environment, and like Adam and Eve in the garden, humans are always curious.

Temptation can arise from the most mundane situations. The following passage from the Bible's book of Proverbs, written thousands of years ago, vividly describes what can happen when husbands and wives are apart for long periods:

> She lays hold of him and kisses him;
> Brazenly she says to him,
> "I have decked my couch with covers

Of dyed Egyptian linen;
I have sprinkled my bed
With myrrh, aloes, and cinnamon.
Let us drink our fill of love till morning;
Let us delight in amorous embrace,
For the man of the house is away;
He is off on a distant journey.
He took his bag of money with him
And will return only at mid-month.

Centuries ago the Talmud offered this blunt advice about adultery: "If the urge comes upon you, go to a nearby town, dress incognito, do what you have to do, and come back home as soon as possible." On the face of it, this matter-of-fact statement in a book of religious authority is shocking and some will find it controversial in its acknowledgment of our desires and its down-to-earth suggestions for dealing with infidelity. However, its purpose is not to encourage adultery. On the contrary, the Talmud realistically concedes that instant gratification, be it sexual or emotional, is a powerful human drive and must be acknowledged if we are to deal with it, wrestle with it, and hopefully overcome it. In this imperfect world, however, declares the Talmud (which takes unflinching account of human weakness), an episode of infidelity should not be allowed to take precedence over our first priority: the family. Protection of the familial relationship enjoys the highest priority. We must minimize the hurt we inflict on others by being as discreet as possible. It is unfair and unwise to humiliate your partner in private with evidence of infidelity, and even worse to allow the humiliation to become public. Fidelity is not inherited; it must be learned and practiced. When this cautionary statement was composed it was adressed to men. Today, with women active in the business world it applies equally to them.

The world is teeming with attractive, tempting women and men. One's mate, however, must be viewed in a separate category— as the chosen person with whom one has embarked on an open-ended journey, fueled by mutual desire and strengthened with the understanding that the relationship is to last a lifetime. A lasting partnership is built on similar values and expectations and buttressed by a joint commitment to raise children and grow old together. The bonds of marriage and family are far more complex than those of an affair because they involve so many more aspects of life, both daily and long-term. The partners share everyday chores, share time with friends and relatives, gather together for holidays and vacations, take care of each other in times of illness. It is helpful to regard fidelity to one's spouse as an ongoing, conscious decision, precisely because we see the vows of marriage being broken all the time. The message to men and women is don't ruin your marriage and break up your family for the sake of fleeting pleasure and instant gratification. Marriage brings with it many responsibilities, but it also offers unique rewards. Dr. Frank Pittman in his book *Private Lies* writes, "In our society monogamy is the ideal and infidelity the primary threat to marriage. It is the deceit . . . the cover-up, the web of lies that are the most difficult for the betrayed partner to come to terms with. It is not so much . . . who one lies *with* as whom one lies *to*."

SOME TWO DECADES AND A book of the Bible pass before we hear about Bathsheba once again. She has survived political crises, social pitfalls, and the personal intrigues in the king's sprawling household, with its competing wives, children, and advisers. David and Bathsheba's love affair and the ensuing cover-up must have been well known to everyone in the gossipy court and could not have made Bathsheba popular among the other wives. Her entry into the king's extended family is not unlike the appearance of the second wife or husband in today's culture. It is in the nature of a polygamous family that the husband's relationships with his many wives will fluctuate and become inevitably diluted, yet Bathsheba manages to sustain her closeness to David. She is the only wife we hear of as having access to the king in his later years, when David is in decline and no longer the national hero he once was.

Though his servants cover him with bedclothes, David shivers, his circulation so poor that nothing can warm him on a cold Jerusalem night. His courtiers say, "Let a young virgin be sought for my lord the king, to wait upon Your Majesty and be his attendant; let her lie in your bosom, and my lord the king will be warm." They search for a likely candidate throughout Israel and find Abishag the Shunammite, an exceedingly beautiful girl whom they bring to the king. She becomes the king's attendant and waits upon him.

In this story the Bible does not shy away from describing the infirmities of old age, even in the case of its greatest hero. Like all mortals, King David becomes frail and old. With clinical objectivity, the biblical narrator describes his diminished virility even as a stunning woman slips beneath the covers next to him in the hope that some of her life force will flow to him. But "the king knew her not"; he did not consummate the relationship.

David's court must swarm with wives and concubines, but

they are not by his side as he lies in his sickbed. Like other elderly people, David craves the human touch more than ever. Only his courtiers hover around him, trying to ensure the comfort of their revered monarch, but David feels isolated and irrelevant to those around him.

Of all the young Bathsheba's communications to David, we know only of three written words: "I am pregnant." These three words, however, were so powerful they shook the kingdom and changed David's life and legacy. Now Bathsheba is older but she displays the same confidence she did in her youth as she takes on the role of advocate for their son, Solomon.

King David, nearing the end of his reign, is no longer in full command as his sons begin their battle for succession. One, Adonijah, son of Haggith, has already proclaimed himself king while his father still lives.

"So Bathsheba went to the king in his chamber. The king was very old, and Abishag the Shunammite was waiting on the king. Bathsheba bowed low in homage to the king; and the king asked, 'What troubles you?' She answered him, 'My lord, you yourself swore to your maidservant by the Lord your God: "Your son Solomon shall succeed me as king, and he shall sit upon my throne."'" The saying "The hand that rocks the cradle rules the world" fully applies to Bathsheba.

After these many years together, Bathsheba has earned easy access to the king. She walks into his bedchamber, secure of her place in David's life. She is not at all threatened by the presence of the desirable Abishag. Though the fiery passion that drew her together with David has cooled, it remains a potent memory. Bathsheba draws on the closeness and loyalty—the last being the rarest quality of all in court life—that she and David nurtured over the years. Bathsheba speaks to him respectfully, and he responds in kind.

Once again, the stakes are high for Bathsheba. The same resolve with which she once spoke on her own behalf as a young woman is summoned now in the cause of their son, Solomon. Not only does she want him to be king, but she realizes that when David dies, any other successor is certain to view Solomon and herself as a threat to his power.

The transfer of power is a recurrent issue in the Hebrew Bible. There, as in most societies, primogeniture is the chosen method for ensuring an orderly transfer. It is not, however, the invariable method. In the Bible primogeniture is repeatedly overturned, as with Jacob and Esau and Joseph and his brothers. David himself is chosen by God to be king even though he is neither King Saul's son nor even his own father's eldest son. It seems possible to suggest that in all of these cases the Bible is counseling merit-based succession.

In the case of the aging David and Bathsheba, the balance of power between them has inevitably shifted, as it did with Rebecca when Isaac grew old. Bathsheba is resolute and energetic, perhaps reminding David of a promise made long, long ago. Might David have consoled his distraught, sobbing wife over the wrenching loss of her firstborn many years earlier by swearing to her that their next son would be king? Is she gambling that he will uphold a vow he may no longer remember, if indeed he made it at all? We do not know if David was sincere at that time, or if the old king is merely playing along with his favorite wife to cover his mental confusion. Or perhaps he made this vow more recently because he believes that of all his offspring, this boy's erudition and wisdom will make him the best successor to lead the nation.

Whatever the reason, David's decisiveness comes to the fore one last time. He names Solomon his successor and, forestalling a challenge from a rival heir, declares an immediate transfer of power. Solomon begins his reign while David is still alive, thus fulfilling David's promise to Bathsheba: "The oath I swore to you by the God of Israel, that your son Solomon should succeed me as king and that he should sit upon my throne in my stead, I will fulfill this very day! . . . Sound the horn and shout, 'Long live King Solomon!' Then march after him, and let him come in and sit on my throne. For he shall succeed me as king; him I designate to be ruler of Israel and Judah."

As his life draws to a close, David gives to Solomon, his chosen heir, a list of instructions ranging from the ruthless elimination of foes to favors for his followers. He bequeaths the wisdom for which Israel's poet king has ever since been admired: walk in God's ways and follow God's laws, commandments, rules, and admonitions "as recorded in the teaching of Moses in order that you may succeed in whatever you undertake and wherever you turn. Then God will fulfill the promise that He made concerning me: 'If your descendants are scrupulous in their conduct and walk before me faithfully, with all their heart and soul, your line on the throne of Israel shall never end!' "

A fortunate mortal, David dies peacefully.

When Solomon ascends to the throne, so great is the esteem in which he holds his mother that when she enters the chamber, "The king rose up to meet her, and bowed down unto her, and sat down on his throne; and he had a throne placed for the queen mother, and she sat on his right."

. . .

THE NARRATIVE DEFTLY RELATES THE changes in the royal relationship from an adulterous one-night stand through murder, mourning, and repentance, marriage, suffering, and consolation, to the coronation of Solomon, arguably Israel's wisest king.

When the story begins, Bathsheba, wife of one of the king's army officers, is the object of the king's lust and entirely dependent on the king's protection. Somehow she successfully changes herself from a mere sexual object into a partner in David's life. David adds her to his collection of wives, not out of political calculations—the usual basis for a royal marriage—but in defiance of it: out of love alone. He must have also respected the way in which she raised their only son, Solomon, because he names Solomon his heir.

As Bathsheba's role evolves, she expresses the more "masculine" characteristic of speaking up assertively, not as a dependent on David's protection, but rather as a woman secure in her place in the royal marriage. When she enters the king's bedchamber and sees Abishag, she must certainly conclude that the girl does not pose a threat to her place in David's life or her status in court while David grows old, lonely, and dependent on the care of strangers. The courtiers are guards, not people who love him. Even Abishag is not emotionally close to him: she's an "employee" with whom David is "not intimate." His private life is full of pain and disappointment, much of it of his own making, with perhaps only the long love affair with Bathsheba to console him.

As for the original triangle, one may speculate endlessly about the motives for each of the three protagonists' every action. Passion and loyalty, self-interest and selflessness are inextricably intertwined. The story is primarily concerned with the abuse and the seductive force of power, manifested through the choices people make. None of the principals in this domestic triangle gets off lightly. Uriah, who refuses the role of the complaisant husband, is killed on the battlefield. Bathsheba must live with her complicity in her husband's death and with the death of a son conceived in sin. But it is David who must bear the most terrible consequence: "the sword shall never depart from your house." David's daughter Tamar is raped by her half brother Amnon; Amnon is murdered by Tamar's brother Absalom in revenge. Absalom's relationship with his father deteriorates from that time on and culminates in his leading a coup against his father and being murdered, against the king's explicit orders, by David's zealous chief of staff, Joab.

David's lust for Bathsheba develops into something close to what we recognize today as romantic love—a passion that takes precedence over political calculations, if not reason itself. The lasting affection that binds the two is of the essence. Bathsheba remains at the side of the sexually impotent David, whose political power is on the wane. As a source of practical intelligence and emotional support, Bathsheba plays a role in shoring up the aging David during his declining years.

Of David's three wives discussed in the Bible, only two are known to have had a profound influence over him, both of them previously married and presumably more mature than the inexperienced and needy Michal, Saul's daughter. Both bring out in him the protector and the leader who enables them to survive and join his court. The first is Abigail, who talks David out of bloody retribution against her husband and their household. The second, Bathsheba, changes the course of history with her rooftop bath; she persuades David to choose their son, Solomon, as his successor over other sons who are older. The respect that Solomon pays his mother after he ascends to the throne suggests her prominence in David's court. Both Abigail and Bathsheba exude courage, the source of their self-confidence. They refuse to accept the status quo when they first meet with David, although their predicaments are perilous. Both are wise and speak their minds. David stops and listens.

TEN

Rape and Revenge: The Story of Tamar

THE BIBLE DOES NOT HIDE shocking secrets in King David's family. "Absalom son of David had a beautiful sister named Tamar, and Amnon son of David became infatuated with her. Amnon was so distraught because of his half sister Tamar that he became sick; for she was a virgin, and it seemed impossible to Amnon to do anything to her."

Amnon has a cousin, a shady courtier named Jonadab, whom the Bible calls "a very clever man." Jonadab asked Amnon, " 'Why are you so dejected, O prince, morning after morning? Tell me!' Amnon replied, 'I am in love with Tamar, the sister of my brother Absalom!' Jonadab said to him, 'Lie down in your bed and pretend you are sick. When your father comes to see you, say to him, "Let my sister Tamar come and give me something to eat. Let her prepare the food in front of me, so that I may look on, and let her serve it to me.' "

Amnon, King David's eldest son, jumps at the idea. "Amnon lay down and pretended to be sick. The king came to see him, and Amnon said to the king, 'Let my sister Tamar come and prepare a couple of cakes in front of me, and let her bring them to me.' David sent a message to Tamar in the palace, 'Please go to the house of your brother Amnon and prepare some food for him.' Tamar went to the house of her brother Amnon, who was in bed. She took dough and kneaded it into cakes in front of him, and cooked the cakes. She took the pan and set out [the cakes], but Amnon refused to eat and ordered everyone to withdraw. After everyone had withdrawn, Amnon said to Tamar, 'Bring the food inside and feed me.' "

The narrator does not describe Tamar's frame of mind as she approaches Amnon's house. When her father David sends her to cook for Amnon, she cannot refuse. But does she suspect Amnon's motives? Did she sense his lustful gaze at court gatherings and family feasts? Does she wonder why her father is oblivious to any possible danger to her? We do not know. Short of disobeying her father and king, she has no choice but to comply with his request.

Tamar may be too innocent to know that the slow preparation of a dish can be highly sensual, a kind of erotic foreplay. Tamar kneads the dough for the cakes before baking them. Amnon's lust for Tamar intensifies as he stares at her graceful movements from his bed. He dismisses the servants, and the two are left alone. We shudder at what we assume is about to take place.

"Tamar took the cakes she had made and brought them to her

brother inside. But when she served them to him, he caught hold of her and said to her, 'Come lie with me, sister.' But she said to him, 'Don't, brother. Don't force me. Such things are not done in Israel! Don't do such a vile thing! Where will I carry my shame? And you, you will be one of the scoundrels in Israel! Please, speak to the king; he will not refuse me to you.' But he would not listen to her; he overpowered her and lay with her by force."

Like most women in her predicament, Tamar lacks the physical strength to escape her attacker, and she relies on her wits, hoping to persuade him to reconsider. She argues and pleads, reminding him of their close family ties. She calls him "brother." She urges him to acknowledge their shared moral heritage, saying, "Such things are not done in Israel!" In desperation, she appeals to his self-interest not to be one of the "scoundrels in Israel."

She goes so far as trying to convince him to legitimize his lust by asking their father to consent to their marriage. Though biblical law forbids marriage between a half brother and half sister, commentators have suggested that her words reflect the fact that such unions were customary among royal families of the ancient Near East. In Egypt in the first century BCE, Cleopatra first married her brother Ptolemy XIV, and after he died, she married their younger brother.

In any event, Tamar grasps at any ploy to stave off Amnon, if only to buy time, but she fails and the inevitable occurs. Amnon rapes his sisters with brute force in what must have been a terrifying and painful ordeal.

Tamar begs him not to compound the evil of the rape by sending her away—the equivalent of banishment. While biblical law offers the "compensation" of marriage to the rape victim, a virgin abandoned by her rapist becomes an outcast whom no one will deign to marry. To modern ears, a law placing the rapist with his victim under one roof sounds brutal, but it was in fact an attempt, however imperfect, to protect a woman who would be otherwise rejected by her community. In an agrarian, patriarchal society in which a woman had no identity independent of marriage, this law tried to make the rapist assume responsibility for his victim's welfare.

But once again, Amnon ignores Tamar's appeal and reveals another ugly facet of his character. "Then Amnon felt a very great loathing for her; indeed, his loathing for her was greater than the passion he had felt for her. And Amnon said to her, 'Get out!' She pleaded with him, 'Please don't commit this wrong; to send me away would be even worse than the first wrong you committed against me!' But he would not listen to her. He summoned his young attendant and said, 'Get that woman out of my presence, and bar the door behind her.'"

Amnon's servant hurries her outside and bars the door. For Amnon, the episode is over. Lust, unlike love, evaporates once it is satisfied. Amnon wants to have nothing more to do with her.

Why does Amnon's lust turn so quickly into "loathing"? He knows he might be caught and punished for what he has done. Her presence becomes intolerable to him because it would be a constant reminder of the hatred and guilt he cannot help feeling. He projects his own revulsion onto her. He further depersonalizes Tamar as "that woman." The victim becomes hateful in the eyes of the aggressor.

HOW DOES ONE BEGIN TO understand the malevolence that prompts Amnon's crime? What leads him to act on an evil urge that other men might fantasize about but not act upon? Why has he no self-restraint? When we meet Amnon, he is tormented by lust for his sister, "for she was a virgin, and it seemed impossible to Amnon to do anything to her." It is precisely Tamar's unavailability—her virginity—that whets Amnon's sexual appetite. In his pathological fantasy she is akin to a walled city that must be breached and conquered.

His friend Jonadab suggests the setup but stops short of indicating that Amnon rape her. Amnon's overheated imagination fills in the blanks.

From the moment the despicable Amnon asks his father David to send Tamar to his house, his moves seem calculated. It is easy to picture him scantily clad, suggestively lounging on his bed, watching Tamar. He is a prince, the king's firstborn, the heir presumptive. Everything comes easily to him. His beautiful half sister is the only thing he has ever wanted that he could not have when he wanted it and the way he wanted it.

All his life Amnon has seen how the court and David's retinue cater to the king's every whim. Did not David catch sight of Bathsheba and take her for himself even though her husband Uriah the Hittite was one of David's loyal officers?

Tamar "was wearing an ornamented tunic, for maiden princesses were customarily dressed in such garments." Once outside the barred door, "Tamar put ashes on her head and rent the ornamented tunic she was wearing; she put her hands on her head, and walked away, screaming loudly as she went."

Her brother Absalom immediately suspects what has happened and asks, " 'Was it your brother Amnon who did this to you? For the present, sister, keep quiet about it; he is your brother. Don't brood over the matter.' And Tamar remained in her brother

Absalom's house, forlorn. When King David heard about all this, he was greatly upset. Absalom didn't utter a word to Amnon, good or bad, but Absalom hated Amnon because he had violated his sister Tamar."

The reader is not spared the raw anguish, humiliation, and pain that the rape victim endures. As Amnon's door bolts shut behind her, Tamar begins to grieve for all she has lost. If she is pregnant, the stigma of illegitimacy will never fade for her or her child. Even if she is not pregnant, no man will marry her. She knows that in the eyes of her community she is "contaminated."

Tamar is stunned by the swift reversal in her status. She entered her brother's home as a cherished princess living a charmed life, but she leaves little better than a harlot, used and discarded by her tormentor. She tears her ornamented tunic bearing the virginal blood of her humiliation, and she staggers home, keening and clutching it around her torn and aching body.

Of those in Tamar's inner circle, only her brother Absalom notices and responds to her distress. At first glance it seems that he makes light of her ordeal, telling her, "He is thy brother; regard not this thing." But in fact Absalom, no fool, knows the situation is delicate, both because Tamar is the king's daughter and because it is her half brother who brought about her ruin.

Absalom's heart is dark with hatred. He begins plotting his revenge, and his admonition to his sister to keep quiet is ominous: "Be silent, for now . . ."

Absalom means to set things straight, but Tamar is not consoled. She sits desolate under his roof, facing a grim future. When her father learns what has happened, he is "greatly upset" but apparently does nothing. The description is maddeningly opaque. Is

David dismayed that his daughter has been raped? That the rapist is his son, and her half brother? That he, her father, put her in a compromising situation that ruined her life? That he never recognized the danger she was facing? Or does he realize that anger, mistrust, and violence doom his family? He may consider all of the above—or none. But what must weigh on his mind is that the son who stoops to rape and incest is expected to inherit the throne. He remains silent, however, as his family barrels toward calamity.

THE READER UNDERSTANDS THAT SOONER or later retribution will follow the rape. "Two years later, when Absalom was having his flocks sheared at Baal-hazor near Ephraim, Absalom invited all the king's sons. And Absalom came to the king and said, 'Your servant is having his flocks sheared. Would Your Majesty and your retinue accompany your servant?' But the king answered Absalom, 'No, my son. We must not all come, or we'll be a burden to you.' He urged him, but he would not go, and he said good-bye to him. Thereupon Absalom said, 'In that case, let my brother Amnon come with us,' to which the king replied, 'He shall not go with you.' But Absalom urged him, and he sent with him Amnon and all the other princes."

However much Absalom presses David, the king refuses to go, with no explanation. David's silence is deafening. Surely he senses what is going to happen, sooner or later, but he is too paralyzed with guilt to give his children any guidance. He does not press Absalom about his intentions toward Amnon, nor does he suggest a course of action, whether punishment or lenience. Is David more concerned with trying to keep up the appearance of family harmony than with Tamar's honor and the need to punish Amnon? The rising hostility between David and his son Absalom over Tamar's rape is becoming apparent. Does David instinctively try to protect Amnon, or is he in denial about the disastrous consequences of his own failure to keep Tamar out of harm's way? In any case, he fails to protect his son, just as he failed to protect his daughter two years earlier.

Absalom orders his servants to watch Amnon and kill him "when he is merry with wine." He tells the servants not to be afraid, "for it is I who give you the order. Act with determination, like brave men!"

The servants carry out Absalom's order, "whereupon all the other princes mounted their mules and fled. They were still on the road when a rumor reached David that Absalom had killed all the princes, and that not one of them had survived. At this, David rent his garment and lay down on the ground, and all his courtiers stood by with their clothes rent."

Jonadab, the well-connected courtier who originally advised Amnon on how to trap Tamar, intervenes once more. Jonadab eagerly suggests to David, in carefully chosen words, "My lord must not think that all the young princes have been killed. Only Amnon is dead; for this has been decided by Absalom ever since his sister Tamar was violated." The underlying message is that Absalom took revenge on Amnon because the king did not carry out his responsibilities to Tamar, his daughter. He did not insist that Amnon marry her as the law on rape demands.

Meanwhile Absalom flees, escaping David's anger at the murder of Amnon.

The narrative returns to David's court in Jerusalem, where

the watchman on duty sees "a large crowd coming from the road." Jonadab sidles up to the king and tells him, "See the princes have come! It is just as your servant said." The princes entered the palace and "broke into weeping; and David and all his courtiers wept bitterly, too."

David's motives for his inaction are unclear. He may have forgiven Amnon because he was his eldest and the crown prince. He may have resisted the idea of a forced marriage, a consequence of rape, because it would harm the reputation of the royal family. But the Bible is silent on his reasons.

In declining Absalom's invitation to the feast while letting Amnon go, David may have been steeling himself—consciously or unconsciously—for Amnon's being punished by his half brother Absalom rather than by himself. Again, David is inadvertently the instrument of his child's misfortune. Amnon pays with his life for raping Tamar.

David is a hero but also human, and an immensely complex character. He is a great army commander and imaginative statesman, one who inspires his people and has the wisdom to choose a neutral site for his capital city. But when it comes to guiding his children, he is a moral coward. After the episode with Bathsheba and Uriah, David seems not to feel he has the moral authority to set limits on his children's behavior. He is inert, even when the situation among his children repeatedly demands the decisive action for which he is so praised in his public life. He does not recognize that Amnon's request represents danger to Tamar; he does not force Amnon to marry Tamar; he does not punish Amnon for raping his sister; he does not prevent Absalom from killing Amnon.

The narrator makes no allusion to Nathan's prophecy that the

sword will never depart from David's house as the inevitable consequence resulting from the murder of Uriah. Unlike Greek tragedy,
the Bible does not attribute human actions to blind fate. Oedipus's
destiny is controlled by an inescapable, amoral fate that predeter-
mines the lives of mortals and even of the gods. No matter how hard
the Greek king tries, he cannot avoid fulfilling the prophecy that he
will kill his father and marry his mother. But the actions and fate of
the characters in the Hebrew Bible are neither predetermined nor
foreordained. Instead, each of us is held to be morally responsible
for our actions. We are not to blame God for our misfortunes. In the
overall spirit of the Hebrew Bible, Nathan's prophecy is a forewarn-
ing of the consequences that derive from our character and our
behavior. The biblical focus is on freedom of choice and its consequent responsibility, even within the context of an overarching divine plan. The rabbinical principle "all is foreseen but freedom of
choice is given" applies to David as it did to Rebecca.

What causes the human sex drive, something inherently
good, to go wrong? We are the only species whose sexuality encompasses our imagination, our conscience, our soul in addition to
our libido. God created sexuality to perpetuate the species, to
strengthen intimacy and trust between the couple. But the outcome
can be joyous and healthy, or miserable and destructive.

It once seemed that with more sexual freedom for both men
and women, men would resort less to rape. They would have more
opportunities to express their sexual feelings with their women
companions and would suffer less sexual frustration. This idea was
wrong. Rape is clearly more about violence and power over the
victim than it is about sex. The world over rape continues to be
employed as a tool in campaigns of terror and subjugation.

In Tamar's time and place, incest and rape carried far more serious social consequences for women than in today's Western societies. The Bible describes Tamar begging Amnon to marry her because after the rape she will be untouchable, unable to marry anyone other than the rapist. After the rape, however, Amnon's lust turns to hate and he refuses to marry her. In fact, Absalom avenges Amnon's refusal to make reparations as much as he avenges the rape.

Today's woman is as traumatized by rape as Tamar was, haunted by shame, fear, guilt, and secrecy. The tragedy of rape still extends beyond the physical consequences, such as pain, pregnancy, and disease, as well as the emotional terror and humiliation of the act itself. It leads to fears of sexual and emotional intimacy. The feelings are even more destructive when rape occurs within the family, which should provide an anchor of safety and trust. These days, however, society is taking more responsibility by instituting hotlines and counseling for the victim, and legal action against the rapist.

Biblical law unequivocally forbids incest, calling it "an abomination," and the prohibitions extend beyond unions between siblings and parents and their children. The book of Leviticus, which discusses the subject at great length, stipulates that the perpetrator is to be cut off from the community. The laws are specific, with consideration for the forced victim. The biblical authors are extraordinarily sensitive to women's vulnerability, and they make it clear that neither God nor a moral people can tolerate such violations of a woman's integrity.

The Bible gives no indication that Amnon wrestles with his conscience. His only concern is the possibility of punishment. On the other hand, Absalom acts within the accepted rules of his time and place. He cannot force Amnon to marry Tamar, but as a brother he is within his rights to kill her rapist. His revenge is violent, but their father David's inaction offers no other recourse.

What about Absalom's motives? Could it be that Absalom is not purely concerned about the rape but also wants to rearrange the order of David's heirs by removing Amnon, the firstborn son? Perhaps he sees himself as a more suitable leader and finds affirmation for this idea in Amnon's rape of Tamar. Or perhaps he knows his sister well and becomes her champion because he knows she did everything in her power to escape this outrage.

THE BIBLE TELLS US NOTHING about the rest of Tamar's life. Her disappearance from the record suggests that she is unable to take her expected place in society by marrying and bearing children. Three thousand years later, Amnon is and will always be "one of the vile ones in Israel," and his crime is considered the most chilling episode in King David's family life.

In a mirror image of Tamar's story, Joseph, Rachel and Jacob's son, is a slave in Egypt in Potiphar's household. Potiphar's wife lusts after him and tries time after time to force him to sleep with her. He refuses. One day, "none of the household being there inside, she caught hold of him by his garment and said, 'Lie with me!' But he left his garment in her hand and got away and fled outside." Nothing has changed from ancient times regarding rape: physical strength is what counts. Unlike the biblical Joseph, women are not physically stronger than their rapists.

Life is seldom fair. As a Greek aphorism puts it, "If a stone falls on an egg, the egg breaks; if an egg falls on a stone, the egg breaks." Given women's lesser physical strength, it behooves them to avoid situations that magnify their vulnerability—from dark parking lots to wild drinking parties. It may be unfair and politically incorrect to impose this entire responsibility on women. However, like it or not, that is the reality and that is the way it will remain until such time as men become as sensitive to the horror of rape as women.

ELEVEN

THE MYSTERY OF THE
QUEEN OF SHEBA

N O ONE KNOWS IF SHE was brilliant or beautiful; even her proper name remains a secret, perhaps forever. For centuries, scholars have argued over the location of her realm—rich in gold, spices, and precious stones, somewhere in eastern Africa or perhaps southern Arabia. But generations of readers and listeners to ancient tales have heard of the powerful Queen of Sheba, who wielded superior skills of diplomacy and held her own in a male-dominated world.

Many of her present-day admirers are not aware that her legend originated in the Bible. Nearly three thousand years ago a mysterious Queen of Sheba visited King Solomon, renowned throughout the world for both wisdom and riches, and the Bible's Book of Kings chronicles their enchanting encounter in thirteen spare verses. The biblical text enumerates no historical or theological consequences to their encounter, and the reason for its inclusion in the canon, not once but twice (in Kings, and then in Chronicles), has always puzzled commentators. Nonetheless, the Ethiopians claim the queen as their own and proudly trace their royal dynasty to her auspicious meeting with the King of Israel.

According to the Bible, "The Queen of Sheba heard of Solomon's fame . . . and she came to test him with hard questions. She arrived in Jerusalem with a very large retinue, with camels bearing spices, a great quantity of gold, and precious stones. When she came to Solomon, she asked him all that she had in mind. Solomon had answers for all her questions; there was nothing that the king did not know, [nothing] to which he could not give her an answer. When the Queen of Sheba observed all of Solomon's wisdom, and the palace he had built, the fare of his table, the seating of his courtiers, the service and attire of his attendants, and his wine service and the burnt offerings that he offered at the House of God, she was left breathless."

The queen's address to the king suggests a mind both sharp and polished: "The report I heard in my own land about you and your wisdom was true. But I did not believe the reports until I came and saw with my own eyes that not even the half had been told me; your wisdom and wealth surpass the reports that I heard. How fortunate are your men and how fortunate are your courtiers, who are always in attendance on you and can hear your wisdom. Praised be God, your God, who delighted in you and set you on the throne of Israel; for God made you king to administer justice and righteousness."

The queen supports her compliments with lavish gifts. "She presented the king with one hundred and twenty talents of gold and a large quantity of spices and precious stones. Never again did such a vast quantity of spices arrive as that which the Queen of Sheba gave to King Solomon."

"King Solomon, in turn, gave the Queen of Sheba everything she wanted and asked for in addition to what King Solomon gave her out of his royal bounty." This penultimate sentence of the episode conveys a rapport between the two rulers going beyond the merely diplomatic.

The mysterious queen's stay in Jerusalem has inspired artists of all kinds. In Western culture the Queen of Sheba is the subject of operas, ballets, and paintings. Her voluptuous figure appears in works by Piero della Francesca, Tintoretto, and Bosch. In the 1959 Hollywood spectacle *Solomon and Sheba*, a sultry Gina Lollobrigida stars as the queen, and a savvy Yul Brynner as the king works hard to measure up to her. In *My Fair Lady*, Henry Higgins boasts to Eliza Doolittle, "I could pass you off as the Queen of Sheba!"

A summit meeting of two rulers was extremely rare in biblical times, as most sovereigns were too fearful of plots back home or in the host country. In this instance a queen comes from the faraway land of Sheba with no history of enmity with the Kingdom of Judah and Israel. Unlike today's heads of state, who drop in for brief, scripted visits, the Queen of Sheba may have stayed for as long as a year. The journey back and forth could alone have taken many months. The biblical text offers no indication of her wearing out her welcome. The laconic last sentence—"Then she and her attendants left and returned to her own land"—suggests that once her goals were achieved, she and her retinue departed.

I picture the queen mounted on her camel, sitting erect and

gazing ahead as the blue haze over the endless stretch of desert beckons to her. The Bible says nothing about her courage, but the rigors of the journey across a succession of notoriously treacherous, trackless deserts—whether in Africa or Arabia or both—would have deterred any but the most determined traveler. If she sets out in the heat of summer, she and her caravan must seek shelter from the day's sun and searing heat. A languid, transient court, the caravan will linger at some welcoming oasis or caravanserai until dusk stirs a breeze, signaling that it is time to set out once again, as torchbearers cut a narrow, luminous path toward Jerusalem, Solomon's capital. A brilliant day may conceal bandits eager to relieve the camels of the goods in their bulging baskets. And the oases that beckon to travelers with their promises of shade and crystal-clear cool water are attended by risks such as exorbitant tolls charged by the local warlord—or ambush.

The Queen of Sheba is a seeker, driven by a desire to meet with Solomon, "test him with hard questions," learn from his wisdom, and see his wealth for herself. Like Eve, unable to resist the tree of knowledge in the Garden of Eden that was "to make her wise," the queen gives rein to her curiosity.

When at last she is face to face with King Solomon, she exudes an aura of wealth, self-confidence, and power equal to his. She uses her royal experience to exercise subtle mastery over what she may also consider an opportunity to forge a commercial and political alliance. She is certainly equal to her formidable host. Although overwhelmed by what she sees, she takes note of the details important to her and her subjects. She sweeps into Solomon's court provisioned with abundant samples intended to demonstrate her kingdom's wealth, express her thanks, and perhaps close a deal. If some of those riches—incense, pungent spices, heaps of gold and jewels—stoke the senses, so much the better.

Her gifts proclaim her realm a major trading power. She brings one hundred twenty talents of gold—a vast fortune in ancient days. The gems and spices are more than opulently generous gifts; they are commodities to be distributed and sold throughout the ancient world. It is unlikely that all the goods originated in her own country. Translucent green emeralds might have come from as far away as India, blue lapis lazuli from Afghanistan, and the bright yellow gold from near Mecca. An accomplished entrepreneur, she has done her homework and so offers goods unavailable or rare in Solomon's kingdom.

The biblical account makes a point of how the luxury of Solomon's household dazzles the Queen of Sheba. But his mind impresses her even more.

Solomon relishes the mental challenge. His wives and courtiers fawn over him, but the Queen of Sheba intrigues him. This most erudite of Israel's kings understands that he must deal with the queen as his equal. It is she who sets the agenda "and asked him all that she had in mind." Some scholars think it likely that, consistent with the custom of the day, her questions are asked in the form of riddles. Solomon must live up to his reputation, and according to the spare biblical account, he does. After they dispense with the formality of the riddles, they may have moved on to issues of concern to their nations: how to establish trade between their realms to enhance the wealth of both.

What the Bible calls her "breathless" reaction to Solomon's lifestyle and intellect is flattering to the king and breaks through the formalities of protocol, enabling her to reach him on a personal level. We can picture the queen, wide-eyed as she anticipates her next move. She compliments him on his accomplishments but without the florid exaggerations of a courtier's flattery. Hers are not the cold machinations of a temptress. She is a political genius who, like Abigail, knows that flattery, used with graceful subtlety and based on truth, lubricates civilized relationships.

Solomon, apparently touched by her response, is impressed that she has come so far to benefit from his knowledge. Who among us can resist a well-honed compliment echoing one's reputation in a far-off land?

The queen is on a mission for her country. She appreciates the leadership qualities she perceives in her host and praises the God of Israel. As smart professional women do today, she sets the boundaries and shrewdly skirts subjects that are too personal or might cause the king to misconstrue her goals. Her expressed admiration is confined to his "wisdom and wealth" and to the God who made him king "to administer justice and righteousness." She says nothing of a personal nature.

True to his reputation, Solomon welcomes his guest with his charm and hospitality. He makes a regal impression as he receives her on his "throne of ivory, overlaid with refined gold." In those "drinking cups of gold" the king's servants must have offered her the finest of wines, a commodity unavailable in the tropical south she comes from.

For once, Solomon can speak with a woman who is his equal in intellect and power, someone not dependent on him, unlike the members of his harem, who number seven hundred wives and three hundred concubines. He must recognize her as an entrepreneur and a ruler of considerable poise firmly in control of her realm.

The blend of power, wit, wealth, and chemistry between the two rulers is irresistible. Though the biblical narrative is silent on the subject, it is easy to imagine a love affair between the desert queen and the urbane king, equals in the throne room as well as the bedchamber. The little we know about the time they spent together gives us leave to infer, surmise, and conjecture. The biblical scribes believed that less is more.

Precisely because of the mutual admiration between the two rulers and the spareness of the biblical text, versions of the Queen of Sheba's visit to Jerusalem were rewritten later in post biblical times and have taken root in the folklore of many cultures. Her character is like a blank canvas on which storytellers through the centuries have painted their images of this powerful, mysterious, and exotic woman. In various traditions she is turned into the founding mother of Ethiopian Christianity, a great monarch, or a rape victim. Many storytellers have invented, on the basis of no evidence, an explicit sexual relationship between the queen and Solomon.

Two famous postbiblical retellings are the Ethiopian *Kebra Negast*, and a version in the Koran. The contrast between the biblical and postbiblical versions are upsetting, not because of the writers' flights of sexual fancy, but because they stress Solomon's cunning and his successful seduction of the powerless queen. Apparently the postbiblical writers cannot tolerate a queen who is intellectually and politically equal to Solomon. They prefer a Solomon who is more powerful than she is and who has the last word. The tales reduce the queen to little more than an uppity woman who dares confront Solomon with "hard questions" and assumes she will depart with her dignity intact.

Nowhere in the world is the Queen of Sheba so revered as in

Ethiopia, because she is the matriarch of a dynasty that ended only in 1975 with the death of Haile Selassie, two hundred thirty-fifth in direct line of descent. The *Kebra Negast* (*Glory of Kings*), the Ethiopian national epic, recounts the journey of the virgin Queen of Sheba to Jerusalem and describes the tension between the queen and the king as decidedly sexual: "He pondered in his heart, 'A woman of such splendid beauty hath come to me from the ends of the earth! What do I know? Will God give me seed in her?' " The queen, unwilling to return to her country in "sorrow, affliction, and tribulation," is determined to keep her virginity.

As her visit in Jerusalem draws to a close, the *Kebra Negast* depicts Solomon as begging her to stay, even proposing marriage. She refuses, but Solomon is undeterred. In the *Kebra Negast*, Solomon and Sheba agree that he will not "take her by force" as long as she does not take "by force anything" that is in Solomon's household. The queen confidently agrees, secure in her wealth and integrity. "Do not imagine that I have come hither through love of riches," she says to him. "Assuredly I have come only in quest of thy wisdom."

The queen sleeps in Solomon's tent. She is awakened by thirst, stoked, according to an Arabic version, by a salty, spicy supper prepared at Solomon's behest. When she reaches across Solomon's bed for the water jug—which he made sure was the only one in the room—he seizes her hand, saying that in taking his water, she broke her oath. She remembers her promise and "gave herself into his embrace willingly."

Later that night Solomon dreams that the sun descends from heaven and hovers over his kingdom for some time but eventually moves on to Ethiopia, where it shines brightly to this day. Solomon realizes to his dismay that Ethiopia, not Israel, is God's chosen land—an African Zion.

The episode of the water jug does not end in marriage. Soon afterward, the Queen of Sheba returns to her country. According to the epic, she is pregnant with Solomon's child Menelik, literally "son of the king," who becomes the founder of Ethiopia's imperial dynasty.

From the point of view of a storyteller, whether in an Ethiopian village or in Hollywood, when a queen visits a king of another land, they must end up making either war or love. The story demands a clash of arms or the mists of romance. For the past three thousand years this is what people have wanted to read and hear, or at least this is what they are conditioned to expect.

The biblical text "everything she wanted and asked for" has been interpreted to mean that she craved Solomon's lust and domination. The accounts depict a sexual relationship in which Solomon, a conniving host, a sleazy predator, wields the power over a virginal Queen of Sheba, who ultimately submits to his sexual desire.

IN THE KORAN, KING SOLOMON'S powers are extended to include astounding wizardry and his attendants include djinns and magic animals as well as the hoopoe bird that serves as his messenger. The hoopoe flies to the Muslim Solomon with news of a wealthy queen in the south who worships the sun, not Allah. Solomon demands that she come to him and submit to him and his God. When the Queen of Sheba balks, Solomon employs various wiles to bring her north. Eventually she arrives and he conjures up in his courtyard a stream that is in fact a mirror. When she enters the palace, she bares her legs to step into what she assumes is a pool of water. Humbled by her mistake, she says she has sinned and submits to Solomon and to Allah.

The reflecting surface affords a peek at her usually covered legs and exposes a malformation, variously described as hooves of an ass or the webbed feet of a goose, or legs covered with a thick coat of hair. The physical defect is an emblem of her spiritual failing. The story comes to an end when she accepts Solomon as her superior who brings her into line, body and soul.

While the postbiblical versions stress Solomon's sexual conquest and strategic superiority, the biblical version stresses equality between the two monarchs. Given what the Bible tells us elsewhere about Solomon, it strikes me as more likely that Solomon's exotic visitor responded to his charm and that their intellectual rapport blossomed into a romantic interlude mutually desired and free of trickery or coercion. Or perhaps her intentions were overtly matrimonial from the beginning. It is possible that the gifts were neither trade nor tribute but her dowry, in accord with the age-old tradition of cementing tribal alliances through marriage. Or she might have perceived in Solomon's wisdom a trait that qualified him to sire the future ruler of her realm. The biblical text tells us only that she did not believe the reports of his wealth and wisdom until she saw them for herself.

The Bible says Solomon gives her "everything she wanted and asked for." This king, who, according to the Bible, "clung to and loved many foreign women," no doubt knew how to respond to most women's desires, including those of his guest, the foreign, intriguing Queen of Sheba. Do respect and equality lead to a deeper romantic appreciation as they spend the days talking and strolling up and down the hills of Jerusalem, perhaps marveling at the "apes and peacocks" in the royal zoo? Does he court her, and does she find him attractive? Does their rapport turn into a love affair?

The biblical chroniclers refrain from describing her talents, character, and whatever transpired between the queen and the king. Nor do they mention the color of her skin, the beauty of her face, or lack of it. They neglect to record if she is descended from Shem, the ancestor of the Semites, or Ham, the ancestor of black Africans. Even more unusual is the omission of her name. The word "Sheba" appears in the Bible as a land, a tribe, or a state, but never as a woman's name. The details of her private life are not revealed.

What we do know about the queen gives us yet another variant on the recurrent biblical themes of boldness in the face of the unknown. Eve leaves Eden. Sarah and then Rebecca leave Mesopotamia for the Promised Land. Rachel, Leah, and Ruth all leave their home and move to a new land. The strong women of the Bible are not afraid to embark on a long journey, a spiritual pilgrimage.

The Queen of Sheba is a remarkable woman for her time. Today women take business trips, explore intellectual and scientific borders, and voyage through space. Women like the Queen of Sheba and her sisters embark on the pathway to their dreams and help realize those dreams for the rest of us. Solomon's guest is an extraordinary leader and entrepreneur. The implied intellectual equality between the two monarchs is high praise for the Queen of Sheba, given Solomon's reputation for wisdom. She is a powerful and alluring personality, and so is the king; they meet as two equal power brokers, comfortable and secure in their roles.

The queen would do well if she were dropped into contemporary life. Her attributes are those to which modern women aspire. She would make an excellent role model and mentor. We know she is not merely clever but wise. She is energetic, physically strong, and curious, eager to learn from others and not inhibited in her quest for knowledge. She feels herself to be equal among equals and perfectly comfortable as a female in a male world. She takes full advantage of her feminine sensibilities while communicating with her peers. And, like Abigail, she does not regard being female as a liability!

TWELVE

JEZEBEL THE WICKED

EZEBEL, THE DEVOTED WIFE OF Ahab, King of Israel, is known as the most wicked woman in the Bible. She and Ahab are the quintessential power couple of ancient Israel. Their story recounts bloody abuse of royal power and even bloodier retribution. The murderous scheme Jezebel designs violates Israel's moral code—Thou shall not murder; thou shall not bear false witness; thou shall not covet thy neighbor's house—which applies to all, king and commoner alike. However, the very concept of morality is unfamiliar to Jezebel, a foreign-born princess raised in a culture where a king has absolute power over his subjects. The Bible suggests that Ahab, the Israelite king, bears a greater share of

responsibility for the murder than his wife because of the tacit role
he chooses to play in the following chilling episode.

Jezebel, daughter of a Phoenician king, Ethbaal, is the wife of
Ahab, who reigned over Israel from 874 to 853 BCE. Raised in the
sophisticated court of seafaring Phoenicians living along the
Mediterranean coast north of Israel, Jezebel is an avid worshiper of
Baal and the other gods of her people. She has a strong sense of
personal entitlement and is more than a match for Ahab.

Ahab—the seventh king after the kingdom of David and
Solomon split into two, Israel in the north and Judah in the south—
grew up in a court where his father, King Omri, cultivated an alliance with the Phoenicians and was attracted to their culture and
worship of Baal, whose phallic altars dotted the landscape of the
region. The Bible records that no sooner had Jezebel arrived in Israel as Ahab's bride than she set up her power base with "the four
hundred fifty prophets of Baal and the four hundred prophets of
[the fertility goddess] Asherah who eat at Jezebel's table." Not one
to be squeamish, Jezebel will soon take to killing the prophets of
the God of Israel.

In his capital city of Samaria (Shomron in the original Hebrew), Ahab has acquired many wives, and the Bible makes mention of "seventy of his descendants." But of all the members of
Ahab's family, the Bible tells us only about Jezebel, who has the
power of a queen although the Bible never calls her that. Following
their marriage, Ahab comes under Jezebel's influence and serves
Baal, a pagan god who at that time presented the greatest challenge
to the faith of Israel. "He erected an altar for Baal in the house of
Baal" in his capital. Ahab's worship of Baal sparks a bloody conflict
between Jezebel and the Israelite folk hero, the prophet Elijah.

The outspoken prophet addresses his people: "How long will you halt between two opinions? If the Lord be God, follow Him; but if it be Baal, follow him." Elijah is speaking of the struggle for survival of Hebrew monotheism, which began with Abraham and Sarah centuries earlier and is practiced by their descendants, small in number and surrounded by followers of the seductive pagan cults.

By marrying Jezebel, King Ahab strengthens his alliance with Phoenicia, in today's Lebanon. He is credited with building fortifications of strategic importance at Hazor in eastern Galilee and in Megiddo in the Jezreel Valley, site of the traditional Armageddon, at the northern end of the Samarian hills. Like his father Omri, Ahab develops the hill country of Samaria, where extensive excavations have disclosed scores of contemporaneous Hebrew inscriptions. But Ahab's impressive national achievements are eclipsed by the personal disaster brought about by his marriage to Jezebel, politically sound though it may have been. Coming under Jezebel's sway and failing to live within the moral code of his faith bring misery in its wake.

The Bible vividly depicts an event affording insight into the workings of Ahab and Jezebel's marriage.

"Naboth the Jezreelite owned a vineyard in Jezreel, adjoining the palace of King Ahab of Samaria. Ahab said to Naboth, 'Give me your vineyard, so that I may have it as a vegetable garden, since it is right next to my palace. I will give you a better vineyard in exchange; or, if you prefer, I will pay you the price in money.' But Naboth replied, 'The Lord forbid that I should give up to you what I have inherited from my fathers!'" According to Israelite law, a family keeps its land in perpetuity.

"Ahab went home dispirited and sullen. . . . He lay down on his bed and turned away his face, and he would not eat. His wife Jezebel came to him and asked him, 'Why are you so dispirited that you won't eat?' "

Ahab recounts his frustrating conversation with the farmer. Jezebel tells him, "Now is the time to show yourself king over Israel. Rise and eat something, and be cheerful; I will get the vineyard of Naboth the Jezreelite for you!"

Ahab lies on his bed facing the wall like a cranky, sullen child. Jezebel knows something serious is bothering him and coaxes her husband into talking and explaining what is on his mind. Like many a contemporary wife, she pelts him with questions until she learns why he is distressed.

Ahab craves what is not his. He does not need yet another plot of land; he covets it only because it adjoins his palace. When he is denied anything, even something that belongs in perpetuity to one of his subjects, he sulks. He knows that what he covets is wrong. His body says it all: he turns his back on the world.

Capable, ambitious, and energetic, Jezebel is ever solicitous of her husband's well-being; she tells him to leave the matter in her hands: "Let thine heart be merry: I will give thee the vineyard of Naboth the Jezreelite."

Jezebel and Ahab are a devoted couple; they understand each other perfectly even without words. They are the type of couple who can finish each other's sentences. They read each other's cues and signals; they play a game with rules clear to both. Like many married couples, they are each familiar and comfortable with the roles they have assigned each other. In domestic matters, Ahab is passive, prompting Jezebel to enact his more aggressive thoughts for him. He trusts his wife completely, and she in turn asserts her power with Ahab's tacit agreement.

Ahab knows better than to ask how Jezebel plans to deal with the recalcitrant farmer, and she knows better than to burden him with details. He trusts her to fulfill his desire to possess the vineyard. By avoiding direct involvement, he hopes to be free of moral responsibility and to keep a political distance from anything underhanded she might do to achieve his goals for him.

In Jezebel's culture, kings enjoy absolute power; nothing is allowed to stand in the path of a king's whim, no matter how unworthy a whim it is. Jezebel is incredulous that Ahab has qualms about satisfying his desire for the vineyard. She tries to rouse him, saying, "Now is the time to show yourself king over Israel." Her concern is that if he has scruples over a matter this small, how can he deal with larger issues? And what kind of image is he projecting to his people?

Jezebel promptly launches a scheme to satisfy her husband. She writes letters in Ahab's name, sealing them with the king's seal, to the elders and nobles who live in Naboth's town. They say: "Proclaim a fast and seat Naboth at the front of the assembly. And seat two scoundrels opposite him, and let them testify against him: 'You have reviled God and king!' Then take him out and stone him to death." By commanding others to commit these crimes at her behest, Jezebel incites perjury and murder so that she can commit theft.

The plan so blatantly violates the norms of his people's faith that Ahab would never undertake it himself. Instead, knowing that what will happen is wrong, he hides behind his wife's skirts to remain ostensibly innocent of her machinations, thus maintaining plausible deniability.

Naboth's townsmen do as they are instructed. Naboth is stoned to death. No one has the courage to stand up and defend the powerless farmer, Naboth, who is one of them. His judges and executioners are his own townsmen, but they assume correctly that Jezebel's actions reflect her husband's wishes.

Naboth stands up to the king for his (own) rights, but his countrymen do not defend him or the law, fearful of disobeying a royal command even when it violates their own ethical principles. To them it is clear that defiance could be as fatal to them and their families as, in fact, it turns out to be for their unfortunate neighbor. The phenomenon of being silenced by terror is all too familiar in our own times.

"As soon as Jezebel heard that Naboth had been stoned to death," she rushes to Ahab to tell him the good news: "Go and take possession of the vineyard . . . for Naboth is no longer alive, he is dead." Unfazed by the sheer cruelty of her action, Jezebel is aware of her husband's sensitivities. She is careful not to describe Naboth's gruesome death but merely emphasizes the point that the vineyard is Ahab's at last. The adoring wife is overjoyed to make her husband happy with the "gift" he so desired. The couple is ready to sit back and enjoy their new vineyard, but as in the story of David and Bathsheba, dire consequences ensue.

As Ahab strolls through his ill-gotten possession, whom should he encounter but Elijah the prophet, "a wild figure of a man, clad only in a leather loincloth and a cloak of hair." Fearless and passionate as always, Elijah means to confront the Israelite king. Familiar with his people's traditions, Ahab knows instantly what Elijah intends to do and realizes he cannot escape. Unlike Jezebel, he is aware that he has sinned and betrayed the values and beliefs of his people. He greets the raging prophet sarcastically: "So you have found me, my enemy?" Ahab shows not a whisper of remorse, only regret that the theft and murder have been discovered.

Just as years earlier the prophet Nathan cried out about King David's affair with Bathsheba and the ruthless cover-up of her husband's murder, so Elijah rails against the couple's injustice toward the innocent and powerless farmer. In this story, as in the case of David and Uriah, biblical ethics deal with relations between the powerful and the powerless. Elijah minces no words and graphically prophesies the punishments to be meted out.

He tells Ahab, "Thus said the Lord: 'Would you murder and take possession?' Thus said the Lord: 'In the very place where the dogs lapped up Naboth's blood, the dogs will lap up your blood too.'" Then Elijah adds, "The dogs shall devour Jezebel in the field of Jezreel."

The biblical account of the couple's demise is brutal in its detail. Ahab is killed in battle against the Syrians when a stray arrow pierces the joint in his armor at the armpit. He orders his charioteer to withdraw, but he cannot because the battle is too fierce. Propped upright in the chariot, the king bravely faces the enemy until he dies at sunset in a pool of blood. The Bible describes his end: "And they washed the chariot by the pool of Samaria, and the dogs licked up his blood." Ahab is buried in Samaria.

Soon afterward, Jehu, a tough army commander, murders the new king, Jehoram, brother of Ahaziah, sons of Jezebel and Ahab. After seizing the throne, Jehu moves against Jezebel.

Ever the proud queen, and knowing what is in store for her, Jezebel makes no attempt to escape or beg for her life but prepares calmly for her death. "Jehu went to Jezreel. When Jezebel heard of it, she painted her eyes with kohl and dressed her hair, and she looked out of the window."

Recall that Michal "looked out of the window" just before her final confrontation with David. In the Book of Judges the dead Canaanite general's mother peered "through the window" wondering "why is his chariot so long in coming?" In each of these episodes a woman looking through a window is a portent of doom.

The makeup serves as a mask to be worn with defiance and dignity, shielding her emotions from the people who are set against her. Jezebel was brought up with a strong sense of decorum and is determined to die on her terms—the royal way.

When Jehu enters the gates, he shouts orders to the eunuchs attending the queen. " 'Throw her down,' he said. They threw her down; and her blood spattered on the wall and on the horses, and they trampled her. Then he [Jehu] went inside and ate and drank. And he said, 'Attend to that cursed woman and bury her, for she was a king's daughter.' So they went to bury her; but all they found of her were the skull, the feet, and the hands. They came back and reported to [Jehu]; and he said, 'It is just as the Lord spoke through His servant Elijah the Tishbite: The dogs shall devour the flesh of Jezebel in the field of Jezreel; and the carcass of Jezebel shall be like dung on the ground, in the field of Jezreel; so that no one will be able to say: "This was Jezebel." ' "

JEZEBEL IS SHREWD, AMBITIOUS, AND strong-willed. What defines her are her lack of scruples and the methodical way in which she carries out Naboth's murder to steal his land. She is immune to the idea of moral struggle, internal conflict, or shame.

She and her husband are completely devoted to each other,

and Ahab is more than her accomplice. With his passivity, he motivates his wife to do his will, knowing that fulfilling his wishes will surely entail murder. Jezebel has become an icon of evil and harlotry. But despite her cruelty to others, Jezebel's role in her marriage to Ahab deserves to be reassessed. Indeed, the Bible depicts Ahab as the greater villain of the two.

Jezebel's upbringing in a court where king and queen wielded unchallenged power helps explain, but hardly justifies, her behavior. She is smart but not wise, cunning but politically insensitive, loyal to her own faith but heedless of the religious beliefs of her husband's subjects and the standards of conduct they expect of their rulers. The Israelites regard her as an intrusive, alien emissary of a foreign culture.

As the king's foreign queen, she ought to have done her homework, which means learning the traditions and customs, faith, values, and strictures of the people she has married into. She does none of these things, too self-absorbed to think that these things matter. It never occurs to her that she must change or adapt in any way. Her husband, the king, fails to offer her the necessary guidance in her new country.

As an Israelite, Ahab understands Naboth's right to his land, the limitations of his own authority as king, and the religious and moral constraints that he, unlike a king in Phoenicia, is expected to observe. Once Naboth is dead, he is also aware that because of Jezebel's trumped-up charges, Naboth's relatives are in no position to protest his appropriation of their family land. Unlike David, who acknowledges his guilt when chastised by the prophet Nathan, Ahab rejects all responsibility for subverting his obligations to his people and their traditions.

When it comes to domestic and personal matters, Ahab is a

weakling compared to his wife. He cedes the initiative to Jezebel and is led by her. He leaves it up to her to work out how to steal the farmer's plot of land, and he builds for Jezebel an altar for Baal. Like Solomon's idol-worshipping wives, Jezebel "turned his heart away after other gods." Thus he relinquishes his duty to his own ethical traditions and allows his personal greed to interfere with the laws of his people.

Jezebel's sense of her Phoenician identity is stronger than Ahab's identification with his Israelite traditions. Ahab has little respect for the unique responsibilities of his faith and moral code, but Jezebel is acting in accord with her own. Therefore with Jezebel there are few expectations and little cause for disappointment. In addition, the collision of her polytheism with Israel's monotheism is part of a very long chain of painful encounters that culminates with the Romans' destruction of Judea some eight centuries later.

Floundering between two worlds, Ahab feels full allegiance to neither. Through inaction Ahab is complicit in his wife's evil behavior. The Bible depicts Ahab as a greater villain than the despised Jezebel, declaring that Ahab did "more to provoke the Lord, the God of Israel, than all the kings of Israel who preceded him."

Jezebel thinks only of material acquisition to benefit herself and Ahab. Unlike the other strong women of the Bible, she defies convention neither for the sake of her family's survival nor for the people whom she and her husband rule. Ahab's responsibilities as an Israelite king are literally foreign to her. As a Phoenician, she assumes she is within her rights to do what she wishes and that there is no price to be paid. The roles in this royal marriage are clearly defined. He is free to pursue foreign alliances, while she attends to the domestic tasks as she sees fit.

Jezebel, not unlike so many of the privileged in our time, acts out of a sense of unbounded entitlement, secure in the close bond and understanding she has with the silent Ahab. Their marriage is a devoted partnership, based on mutual support, trust, and loyalty, but unlike that of Abraham and Sarah, it is devoted to greed and instant gratification.

Once Jehu had seized power Jezebel realizes that her days are numbered and she prepares to meet her death with courage in accord with the royal code of her native land. Jehu is so threatened by her power that he kills her brutally even before his rule can be established. She goes to her death hated by the people, without ever comprehending the source of their outrage. But Ahab, the Israelite king, had no such excuse.

It is Elijah who emerges as the voice of conscience. Fearless of possible consequences, he roundly condemns the evil complicity between Jezebel and her husband and the conspiracy of silence that ties the townspeople to Jezebel. It is the prophet alone who speaks in the name of God to remind everyone, powerful and powerless, of the duties of morality and compassion.

THIRTEEN

Two Tales of Seduction

T
HE BIBLE NAMES TWO BOOKS after outstanding
women. The first one is Ruth, a foreigner who chooses to become
a Hebrew like her husband and his family. The second is Esther,
a Jewess living centuries later in exile in Persia, who finds herself thrust into
making a life-and-death choice for her people. Issues of identity are central
to the lives of both women.

Both Ruth and Esther use seduction as a means of survival in a male-
dominated world. The biblical narrative suggests nothing underhanded or
shameful about the women's use of their sexual powers. It presents the art of
seduction candidly and sympathetically. Again in these stories the biblical
scribes seem to empathize with the women and display a deep understanding
of their circumstances.

RUTH

RUTH'S STORY OPENS WITH YET another biblical famine, this one in the land of Judah. Elimelech and his wife, Naomi, flee their home in Bethlehem (a name which, ironically, means "House of Bread" in Hebrew) and head for Moab, a land east of the Dead Sea. Elimelech dies, and Naomi is left with their two sons, who later marry Moabite women, one named Orpah and the other Ruth. After both sons die without siring a child, Naomi decides to return home.

Naomi starts out on her journey with her two daughters-in-law but soon changes her mind. " 'Turn back, each of you to her mother's house. May the Lord deal kindly with you, as you have dealt with the dead and with me! May the Lord grant that each of you find security in the house of a husband!' She kissed them farewell. They broke into weeping and said to her, 'No, we will return with you to your people.'

"But Naomi replied, 'Turn back, my daughters! Why should you go with me? Have I any more sons in my body who might be husbands for you? Turn back, my daughters, for I am too old to be married.' " She urges them to stay in their own land rather than to follow her into an uncertain future.

"They broke into weeping again, and Orpah kissed her mother-in-law farewell. But Ruth clung to her." Naomi tells Ruth to follow her sister-in-law and return to "her people and her gods."

"But Ruth replied, 'Do not urge me to leave you, to turn back and not follow you. For wherever you go, I will go; wherever you lodge, I will lodge; your people shall be my people, and your God my God. Where you die, I will die, and there I will be buried. Thus and more may the Lord do to me if anything but death parts me from you.' " Ruth's commitment and love are unconditional. With these well chosen and emotional words Ruth covers all of the possible contingencies.

Ruth is considered the first convert to Judaism mentioned in the Bible. She converts despite being repeatedly turned away by Naomi, and she chooses Judaism because she appreciates the practical implications of its humane ethical principles as practiced by her mother-in-law. She has grown to love Naomi, who has always shown her kindness and consideration. Ruth not only takes her late husband's faith, she commits herself to his family, community, and history. In particular, she commits herself to be companion and succor to her elderly mother-in-law, who would otherwise be alone and without resources in an inhospitable world. The passionate words of Ruth's declaration are used today in the contemporary ritual of conversion to Judaism.

Ruth follows Naomi to Bethlehem. The Bible notes that upon their arrival, "the whole city buzzes with excitement over them. The women said, 'Can this be Naomi?' "

Naomi, inconsolable, takes no pleasure in the joy with which she is welcomed. Her lot is "very bitter," she says. "I went away full, and the Lord has brought me back empty." Naomi is too disheartened to seek out her kinsmen, among them Boaz, a relative of her dead husband and "a man of substance."

The two women arrive in Bethlehem at the beginning of the barley harvest. Ruth wants to go "to the fields and glean among the ears of grain, behind someone who may show me kindness." (Local custom, codified in the Bible, obliges landowners to allow the poor to collect seeds that fall on the ground.) Naomi gives her permission, so Ruth goes out and follows in the footsteps of the reapers.

Seemingly with tongue in cheek, the Bible notes "as luck would have it, it was a piece of land belonging to Boaz." When Boaz goes to inspect the harvest, he notices Ruth and asks the servant in charge of the reapers, "Whose girl is that?" The servant replies, "She is a Moabite girl who came back with Naomi from the country of Moab and asked for permission to glean." The servant adds that "she has been on her feet ever since she came this morning. She has rested but little in the hut." The servant is referring to Leviticus 19, in which it states, "When you reap the harvest of your land, you shall not reap all the way to the edges of your field, or gather the gleanings of your harvest. . . . You shall leave them for the poor and the stranger: I the Lord am your God."

Doubtless recognizing the name of Naomi, Boaz approaches Ruth and says, "Listen to me, daughter. Don't go to glean in another field. Don't go elsewhere, but stay here close to my girls. Keep your eyes on the field they are reaping, and follow them. I have ordered the men not to molest you. And when you are thirsty, go to the jars and drink some of [the water] that the men have drawn."

The narrative says that Ruth "prostrated herself with her face to the ground." But then she is bold enough to ask Boaz, "Why are you so kind as to single me out, when I am a foreigner?" Is she fishing for a compliment, or perhaps longing for male attention after years of widowhood? And does Boaz's order to his men not to molest Ruth mean that other gleaners were indeed molested?

Boaz, well informed about events in far-off Moab, tells her, "I have been told of all that you did for your mother-in-law after the death of your husband, how you left your father and mother and the land of your birth and came to a people you had not known before. May the Lord reward your deeds."

Ruth replies, "You are most kind, my lord, to comfort me and to speak gently to your maidservant."

From the moment Boaz notices Ruth, he singles her out for attention. She responds warmly, emphasizing her gratitude for his offer of protection. Seizing her chance, she impresses Boaz with her modesty. Yet at the same time she is not afraid to speak up. Ruth wants to make sure that Boaz will not forget her.

At mealtime Boaz invites Ruth to join the reapers. "He handed her roasted grain, and she ate her fill and had some left over." When she gets up to return to work, Boaz orders the workers to let Ruth glean and, in addition, to pull up some stalks and leave them for her to harvest. The landowner is solicitous and caring and his small acts of kindness are not lost on Ruth.

She works in the fields until evening, then carries what she has gathered to her mother-in-law. Naomi, surprised by the volume of Ruth's take, asks her, "Where did you work? Blessed be he who took such generous notice of you!"

Ruth tells her the man's name is Boaz. Naomi says that Boaz is "related to us; he is one of our redeeming kinsmen." It strikes Naomi that Boaz might well decide to provide an heir for his kinsman, Ruth's late husband.

Naomi devises a plan. She may call herself old and bitter, but her survival instincts are unimpaired, and she loves her daughter-in-law. While she is "too old to be married," she recognizes a very rare opportunity for the widow Ruth to marry their thoughtful kinsman and begin a new life of dignity and prosperity. Furthermore, Ruth's marriage to Boaz would ensure that the name of Naomi's son does not disappear and she, Naomi, will be blessed with a grandchild.

"Daughter, I must seek a home for you, where you may be

happy," Naomi tells Ruth. No longer a passive victim of misfortune, Naomi lays out an elaborate strategy for securing "kinsman Boaz" as a husband for Ruth. Familiar with the grains of the land and the sequence of their harvest, Naomi knows that "he will be winnowing barley on the threshing floor tonight." Her instructions to Ruth are timeless and universal: "Bathe, anoint yourself, dress up, and go down to the threshing floor." Naomi, more worldly than her daughter-in-law, cautions, "But do not disclose yourself to the man [Boaz] until he has finished eating and drinking. When he lies down, note the place where he lies down, and go over and uncover his feet and lie down. He will tell you what to do."

Trusting her mother-in-law's experience and wisdom, and without a moment's hesitation, Ruth responds, "I will do everything you tell me."

Ruth walks over to the threshing floor and does as she was told. "Boaz ate and drank, and in a cheerful mood went to lie down beside the grain pile. Then she went stealthily and uncovered his feet and lay down. In the middle of the night, the man gave a start and pulled back—there was a woman lying at his feet!"

Boaz is startled. "Who are you?" he asks. She replies, "I am your handmaid Ruth. Spread your robe over your handmaid, for you are a redeeming kinsman."

Boaz, a wealthy landowner well into his maturity, must have entertained overtures from eligible women in the community. Nonetheless, he is touched that this young woman whom he finds attractive expresses interest in him. In his first encounter with Ruth he called her "daughter," because she is young enough to be that. He now confesses, "Your latest deed of loyalty is greater than the first, in that you have not turned to younger men, whether poor or rich.

And now, daughter, have no fear. I will do in your behalf whatever you ask, for all the elders of my town know what a fine woman you are."

Boaz is ready to serve as a redeeming kinsman.

But for the moment he gently and protectively advises Ruth to lie at his feet and to rise before dawn or, as the Bible tactfully phrases it, "before one person could distinguish another." Concerned for her reputation, he thinks, "Let it not be known that the woman came to the threshing floor." He is also concerned with her welfare, reminding her to take some food with her. He fills the shawl she wears with "six measures of barley, and he put it on her back."

Throughout history, and certainly today, an offer of food represents an expression of love. Whether for our children, our spouses, our friends, when we prepare food, mere nutrients are transformed into a gift that signifies our giving of ourselves through our time, effort, and care.

Throughout the Bible, providing food is a recurrent motif in the love stories of Eve, Sarah, Abigail, Esther, and even Jezebel. Biblical women offer food to men to comfort and to entice them; it is a currency of their affection. In her instructions, Naomi tells Ruth to be sure that Boaz has eaten his dinner and will be in the best of moods and open to Ruth's advances afterward. However, at this point in their relationship, it is Boaz who for the second time makes sure Ruth has enough barley for her and Naomi.

Ruth is aware that her boldness might easily meet with rejection and shame. She might be scolded and sent away. Her reputation might be destroyed. But Boaz, as Naomi's relative, is charged with the family's welfare, and according to local law and custom, even a distant relative is encouraged to marry a childless widow and thus perpetuate a dead man's family line. So Ruth summons her courage in the hope that Boaz will himself fulfill his obligation as a redeeming kinsman.

By asking Boaz to spread his robe over her, Ruth indicates to Boaz that she is available for marriage. Spreading his "robe"—literally the wing of his cloak—over her would imply the protection of formal marriage. As Ruth moves closer to him for warmth, her physical proximity suggests that sensual pleasure would be part of their future life together.

Ruth and Boaz lie on the threshing floor surrounded by sheaves of newly cut barley stalks and breathing in their fresh scent. The Bible is silent about what transpires between them during that harvest night rich with promise, but the imagery of ripened fertility and prosperity for the future is suggestive.

Naomi's plan bears fruit. Boaz promises Ruth he will do all he can in accordance with the law. True to his word, Boaz soon appears before the elders and other townspeople and claims Ruth as his wife, "so as to perpetuate the name of the deceased upon his estate, that the name of the deceased may not disappear from among his kinsmen and from the gate of his home town." Boaz also restores to Naomi her husband's land and status in the community. The story culminates in a betrothal, and the three protagonists— the landowner, the young widow, and her mother-in-law, united by their common faith in Providence—find love and fulfillment.

Ruth bears Boaz a son, who is counted as Naomi's grandson. His name is Obed, and he will be the father of Jesse, who in turn will sire David, the future king of Israel. Despite Ruth's unorthodox method of securing a husband, or perhaps because of it, she ranks high in the memory of her adopted people as the great-grandmother of its fabled warrior-poet, who for forty years ruled a united monarchy from Jerusalem.

THE SEDUCTION SCENE PLAYED OUT ON the threshing floor is between two decent and morally responsible people. The biblical scribes do not frown on Ruth's sexual boldness, nor do they assume a self-righteous posture. Recognizing the need for a gentle nudge to a male of the species who happens to be a man of integrity, they do not take exception to any part of Naomi's plot. The Bible accepts human nature and works with it rather than against it.

In piecing together a book that is both a history of a people and its moral code, the Hebrew Bible esteems women who refuse to surrender to misfortune but marshal whatever resources they have available to defy what others view as inescapable fate. Ruth is a foreign, childless widow who, by operation of the levirate law, gains an honored position in society; this is the same levirate law used by the first Tamar in the book of Genesis, who tricks her father-in-law, Judah, into siring a child for her dead husband. These women are alert to the rare appearance of opportunities for them to achieve justice, and they have the courage to act on their convictions.

Part of the attraction of the book of Ruth derives from the appealing qualities of the two women, who are bound in a friendship that survives the loss of husbands and fortune. Naomi defies the conventional portrayal of the reviled mother-in-law. She is an exemplar of a wise and tactful older relative. Her fondest wish for her daughter-in-law is "security in the house of a husband," and she is quick to help Ruth seize an opportunity to achieve that objective.

Naomi's detailed advice to Ruth is as useful to women today as it was thousands of years ago.

As Tolstoy says, "Women are well aware that what is commonly called sublime and poetical love depends not upon moral qualities, but on frequent meetings and on the style in which the hair is done up, and on the color and cut of the dress." Naomi tells Ruth to make herself as attractive as possible and to approach Boaz when he is relaxed, comfortable, and well fed. This advice is, however, first and foremost, predicated on the choice of an honorable, responsible man who has the qualities of a caring and trustworthy mate.

While the tale ends with Ruth's remarriage to Boaz, the love and friendship between the two women endures. After Ruth gives birth to Naomi's grandson, the town's women congratulate Naomi and express their admiration for "your daughter-in-law who loves you, who is more to you than seven sons." In biblical times as today, the bonds between women are a source of primal strength to which they instinctively turn in times of joy and times of trouble.

This is a story of merits recognized and good deeds repaid; tragic losses are followed by tender love, and righteous lives are rewarded by God and man. From famine to plenty, from the deaths of the three men of the family to the appearance of a loving kinsman and the birth of a son, the book of Ruth is a rare biblical story without villains and with an unconflicted happy ending.

ESTHER

THE BOOK OF ESTHER IS set in the fourth century BCE, when a people by then identified as Jews are exiled in Persia, where they live as a vulnerable minority. The libidinous Persian king Ahasuerus—probably the ruler known today as Xerxes I—wields absolute and tyrannical power over one hundred twenty-seven provinces extending from Ethiopia to India.

Esther—the name means "star" in Persian—is an orphan who has been adopted by her cousin Mordecai, a Jew of the tribe of Benjamin. She joins the pool of what the Bible calls "beautiful young virgins" selected from all the king's provinces. Ahasuerus will choose one of them to replace Queen Vashti, who was banished for disobeying his command to appear before the court in the nude, save for a diadem "to display her beauty to the people and the officials; for she was a beautiful woman." The king is "merry with wine" and so are the guests, who have been drinking for seven days. Queen Vashti's defiance—she was perhaps an early feminist—results in her banishment from the court and she "shall never enter the presence of King Ahasuerus."

Esther gains special favor in the palace of Shushan, where she and the other virgins are assembled in preparation for their first appearance before the king. Although Esther is isolated from the outside world in the harem, every day her wary adoptive father Mordecai walks in front of the palace gates "to learn how Esther was faring and what was happening to her." Following Mordecai's opaque instructions, the ever-obedient girl does not reveal "her people or her kindred." Mordecai is a forerunner of the "court Jew" in medieval Europe who learns to survive by his wits in a hostile environment, advising the king while also attending to the needs of his imperiled fellow Jews.

During the obligatory year Esther spends in the harem before being summoned to the king, she learns about the workings of the court and the ways of the concubines. She is beautified, receiving treatments that include "six months with oil of myrrh and six months with perfumes and women's cosmetics." The royal treatment brings to mind some of what Sarah, Abraham's wife, must have experienced when taken into Pharaoh's harem. The virgins are cloistered for that long so the eunuchs overseeing the harem can be confident that none of them is pregnant or diseased before the king deigns to lie with her. The girl would then "go on the evening and leave in the morning. . . . She would not go again to the king unless the king wanted her, when she would be summoned by name." (These girls in Ahasuerus's harem fare better than those in a later story in *The Arabian Nights*. In that famous tale the girl is killed the morning after the king has deflowered her, and a fresh virgin is brought to him in the evening—a harsh but effective system of birth control.)

In the seventh year of Ahasuerus's reign Esther is called before the king. After one night "the king loved Esther more than all the other women, and she won his grace and favor more than all the other virgins. So he set a royal diadem on her head and made her queen instead of Vashti."

At about the same time, while lurking around the palace gate, Mordecai learns of a conspiracy. He tells Queen Esther about two eunuchs who are plotting to do away with the king. She immediately reports the tip to the king in Mordecai's name. The charge is investigated and found to be true. The two eunuchs are impaled on stakes.

Shortly afterward the king promotes a courtier named Haman to the post of grand vizier and "seated him higher than any of his fellow officials. All the king's courtiers in the palace gate knelt and bowed low to Haman, for such was the king's order concerning him. But Mordecai would not kneel or bow low."

Haman is furious. Informed that Mordecai is Jewish, "Haman plotted to do away with all the Jews, Mordecai's people, throughout the kingdom of Ahasuerus." Without disclosing the identity of the group who enrages him, Haman asks for the king's permission to issue an edict against "a certain people, scattered and dispersed among the other people in all the provinces of your realm, whose laws are different from those of any other people and who do not obey the king's laws." The king accepts the vizier's recommendation, and soon a royal edict is drawn up instructing officials in all the provinces to "destroy, massacre, and exterminate all the Jews, young and old, children and women, on a single day on the thirteenth day of the twelfth month—that is, the month of Adar."

When Mordecai hears the decree, he tears his clothes and puts on "sackcloth and ashes. . . . In every province that the king's command and decree reached, there was great mourning among the Jews, with fasting, weeping, and wailing, and everybody lay in sackcloth and ashes."

Mordecai, however, considers all possible means to avert the disaster.

Through one of the eunuchs assigned to Esther, Mordecai informs her of the decree and orders her "to go to the king and to appeal to him and to plead with him." Esther is "greatly agitated"; she sends a reply to Mordecai explaining that any person who enters the king's presence without being summoned is punished by death. Who would dare take such a risk? She confides that the king has not summoned her for the past thirty days, leaving her to wonder whether his desire for her has waned.

Mordecai is harsh and uncompromising: "Do not imagine that you, of all the Jews, will escape with your life by being in the king's palace. On the contrary, if you keep silent in this crisis, relief and deliverance will come to the Jews from another quarter, while you and your father's house will perish. And who knows, perhaps you have attained to royal position for just such a crisis." These words foreshadow the vulnerability of Jews in the Diaspora. In the midtwentieth century, Jews who thought they might for one reason or another be exempt from Nazi extermination usually found themselves to be wrong. Even mistresses to Nazis ended up in the gas chambers.

Esther's next message to Mordecai demonstrates new resolve: "Go, assemble all the Jews who live in Shushan, and fast in my behalf; do not eat or drink for three days, night or day. I and my maidens will observe the same fast. Then I shall go to the king, though it is contrary to the law; and if I am to perish, I shall perish!"

Esther relies on her beauty and intelligence and uses the only tools at her disposal—sex and food—to avert the evil decree. Astutely surmising that her only chance is to appeal to the king's limitless appetite for food, wine, and women, she develops a plan. With great care she grooms herself and puts on royal apparel. With the eunuch's help she drenches herself with perfumes and oils. Uninvited, she enters the king's throne room.

Ahasuerus is delighted to see his queen and bids her to touch the tip of the golden scepter he is holding, which contemporary psychologists interpret as a phallic overture. "What troubles you, Queen Esther?" the king asks in his most unctuous voice. "And what is your request? Even to half the kingdom, it shall be granted you."

Esther responds by inviting the king and Haman to a feast she has prepared. After wine and food, the king again asks Esther what she wishes for. She invites them both to yet another feast the following day and promises then to do the king's bidding, all the while intensifying his lust and curiosity. The king, enthralled, readily accepts her promise of future diversions.

At the second feast Esther again plies the king and Haman with food and wine. In the presence of Haman, Queen Esther holds the king to his promise to grant her any wish. She takes her life into her hands by revealing her Jewish identity. At this turning point in her life she says, "If Your Majesty will do me the favor, and if it pleases Your Majesty, let my life be granted me as my wish, and my people as my request. For we have been sold, my people and I, to be destroyed, massacred, and exterminated."

When the king learns that Haman is the adversary plotting the death of Esther and her people, he orders that Haman be impaled on the very stake the vizier has prepared for Mordecai because of Mordecai's refusal to bow to him. On the very day Esther's people were to be exterminated, they gain power and triumph over their persecutor, as the king grants the Jews permission to defend themselves. The Bible notes that "in every province and in every city, when the king's command and decree arrived, there was gladness and joy among the Jews, a feast and a holiday."

GOD IS NEVER MENTIONED IN the book of Esther, which makes its inclusion in the canon puzzling. Nor does the story reflect Jewish religious practice other than the ritual of fasting. However, God's unseen hand is behind the events. For Mordecai points out to Esther that her presence in the court may not be accidental, and that she has risen to become queen "for just such a crisis."

Year after year, on the thirteenth day of the Hebrew month of Adar, Jewish communities the world over commemorate Esther's triumph in a joyous, raucous holiday known as Purim. Young and old dress up and jeer each time Haman's name is mentioned during the reading of the Scroll ("Megillah") of Esther, as it is traditionally referred to. Little girls with painted cheeks and mouths smeared with lipstick vie for the right to play the lovely queen and boys swagger as Mordecai, King Ahasuerus, or even the villain Haman.

However, the story imparts several sobering messages. Haman's character cautions us that hatred can become obsessive, in this case turning a private grudge (against Mordecai) into a plan for a holocaust against an entire people. By the end of the tale Haman is impaled and the Jews are free to defend themselves. They will not be so fortunate millennia later when there will be no Esther to save them.

The story reflects the hazards of placing absolute power in the hands of a ruler, no matter how well intentioned. The monarch in this story deflowers scores of virgins and executes anyone who enters the throne room uninvited. Had he not been deterred, he would have killed all his Jewish subjects—probably without losing a night's sleep. Yet it seems he was not a particularly evil man. Rather his case illustrates the maxim that "power tends to corrupt; absolute power corrupts absolutely." Our era is replete with absolute rulers who are no more accountable for their actions than King Ahasuerus was in the fourth century BCE.

The character of Mordecai, Esther's uncle, raises troubling questions. Would he have sent his daughter, his own flesh and blood, to compete in a beauty pageant which might lead her to spend the rest of her life in the king's harem? Would he have ordered his own daughter to take a forbidden initiative with the monarch at the risk of her life? Or was he less emotionally invested in Esther, an adopted relative, an orphan totally dependent on him? On the other hand, did Mordecai and his people have any option? So much was at stake.

This book of the Bible is named for Esther, as well it should be. When we first meet Esther, she is a submissive, compliant orphan. She is also a foreign woman, powerless and marginalized, living in the vast Persian Empire. Obedient to Mordecai's instructions, she must live with the humiliation of having to hide her true identity. Always dependent on others, she has learned to survive by currying the favor of those in power through obedience, servility, and pliability.

The turning point in Esther's character development comes when she faces a terrible choice between protecting her own life by lying low and saying and doing nothing, and taking action and confronting the king with a plea in behalf of her people, thereby revealing her Jewish identity. The narrative suggests that her self-esteem and self-reliance grow as she relieves herself of the burden of her secret. Thenceforth she is free to be herself. We witness her evolution into a woman of action who will employ her courage, sexuality, and political intelligence to gain freedom and justice for her people.

Esther's achievement suggests that even an inexperienced young woman in a dangerous and complex situation can, if she possesses the moral fiber, summon the strength to rise to the challenge of a rabbinical observation written centuries later: "He who behaves like a lamb is devoured like a lamb."

"If I perish, I shall perish!" With these poignant words Esther transformed herself from a mere celebrity to a timeless biblical heroine.

FOURTEEN

THE SONG OF SONGS

THE SONG OF SONGS, ALSO known as the Song of Solomon, offers a remarkable variation on the role of sex and desire in the lives of the biblical women. It is a beautifully written celebration of mutual passion and sensuality between a woman and a man, with emphasis on the woman's longings and yearnings. It differs from all the other biblical stories in that the woman is not cast in her traditional roles of wife, mother, sister, or in-law. Nor is she depicted as dealing with infertility, family dynamics, or the difficulties women face in a patriarchal power structure. She is, in contrast, a young woman in love.

The dominant voice in the poem belongs to the woman Shulamite, who opens the Songs:

Oh, give me of the kisses of your mouth,
For your love is sweeter than wine.
Your ointments yield a sweet fragrance,
Your name is like finest oil—
Therefore do maidens love you.
Draw me after you, let us run!

And concludes them as well:

O you who linger in the garden,
A lover is listening;
Let me hear your voice.
"Hurry, my beloved,
Swift as a gazelle or a young stag,
To the hills of spices!"

The poems are about the wonder of the "other," the longing "to know" and to be known. As the two lovers take turns speaking, their lines create an ode to sensual love that emphasizes their equality and utter delight in each other. The poems are meticulously crafted to convey the sheer, spontaneous, and unself-conscious joy of the lovers. The eroticism in the Songs is expressed with vivid imagination, and one is struck by the spirit of generosity and admiration the lovers feel and articulate to and about each other. Indeed, each seems to be competing to be more ardently complimentary than the other.

"ALL THE SCRIPTURES ARE HOLY, but the Song of Songs is the Holy of Holies," the great sage Rabbi Akiva wrote almost two millennia ago. The Song of Songs, the Bible's treasure trove of love poems, is tucked away amid the thirty-nine books of the Hebrew Bible. Barely eight chapters long, it is one of the shortest books of the Bible.

The eroticism of the Song of Songs comes across as refreshingly innocent and wholesome, especially when contrasted with the crude sexual images and language so pervasive in contemporary Western culture. The tender romanticism of the poems surprises and may even embarrass today's teenagers, accustomed to the throbbing rhythms and raw, confrontational lyrics of much of popular music—often crude and denigrating of women. Consider here the unabashed yearnings of the young woman in the Song of Songs desiring to be close to her lover:

Upon my couch at night
I sought the one I love—
I sought, but found him not.
"I must rise and roam the town,
Through the streets and through the squares;
I must seek the one I love."

You are fragrant,
You are myrrh and aloes.
All the young women want you.

Take me by the hand, let us run together!

My lover, my king, has brought me into his chambers.
We will laugh, you and I, and count
Each kiss, better than wine.

Unlike the other books of the Bible, the Songs have nothing to do with history, codes of ethics, or the establishment of a people. They can be taken literally or read as allegories. When the young man refers to the woman as a "sealed garden" in the "vineyard," the passage can be understood as the location of their encounter or the images may be taken as a reference to her anatomy. "Honey and milk under your tongue" may be read on several levels. The reader will derive the most enjoyment by responding to the poems emotionally, letting his imagination run free in deciphering the voluptuous metaphors.

The poem speaks in several voices: the young woman Shulamite; her brothers, who fret about their young sister ("What shall we do for our sister when suitors besiege her?"); the daughters of Jerusalem, who tease the young woman and badger her for details; and Shulamite's ardent lover.

Where has your lover gone,
O beautiful one?
Say where he is
And we will seek him with you.

The poem is the outstanding example of the Bible's celebration of human sexuality as an integral, positive aspect of life and God's gift to His children. Of course, depictions of desire, sexual jealousy, love, and lust run through the stories of Eve, Sarah, Rebecca, Jacob's wives, and Ruth, to name only a few, but the Song of Songs is the Bible's most lushly sensual treatment of sexuality.

In the course of the eight poems the lovers come together and separate, lose each other, then gravitate toward each other again. At times it is difficult to distinguish which of the lovers is speaking because the lines are entwined and the boundary between them is blurred. The lovers become "one flesh," they part, and they join together, getting to "know" one another more deeply, in an echo of Eve's sharing of the fruit of knowledge with Adam in the Garden of Eden.

In most of the poem it is the woman who reaches out with longing to her lover, reflecting the elusive nature of love and the yearning always to be closer, emotionally, spiritually, to the loved one. In the Songs, there is no shame in loving, in intimacy, or in expressing sexual desires.

Their trysts take place in the spring, when crocuses and lilies arise from the bare ground. The lovers extol the beauty of the natural world as a garden free from guilt or shame. The lover describes his beloved as an "enclosed garden," a "hidden well," an intimate place not accessible to others but available only to him.

> *How beautiful you are, my love,*
> *My friend! The doves of your eyes*
> *Looking out*
> *From the thicket of your hair.*
> *Your hair*
> *Like a flock of goats*
> *Bounding down Mount Gilead. . . .*
>
> *A crimson ribbon your lips—*
> *How I listen for your voice!*
>
> . . . .
>
> *Your breasts are two fawns,*
> *Twins of a gazelle,*
> *Grazing in a field of lilies.*

Before day breathes,
Before the shadows of night are gone,
I will hurry to the mountain of myrrh,
The hill of frankincense. . . .
An enclosed garden is my sister, my bride,
A hidden well, a sealed spring. . . .

The young woman's moods shift between passion and co-
quetry, yearning and self-reproach. Here she reveals the elusive nature of love and her determination to find her lover, who has
slipped away with the help of her girlfriends.

I opened to my love
But he had slipped away.
How I wanted him when he spoke!

I sought him everywhere
But could not find him.
I called his name
But he did not answer. . . .

Swear to me, daughters of Jerusalem!
If you find him now
You must tell him
I am in the fever of love.

The young woman summons images of strength to describe
her lover. He is said to be as strong and erect as a cedar of Lebanon,
while he is also gentle and tender.

His head is burnished gold,
The mane of his hair
Black as the raven.

His arm a golden scepter with gems of topaz,
His loins the ivory of thrones
Inlaid with sapphire,
His thighs like marble pillars
On pedestals of gold.

Tall as Mount Lebanon,
A man like a cedar!

His mouth is sweet wine, he is all delight.
This is my beloved
And this is my friend,
O daughters of Jerusalem.

The poem's climax in the last section is an eloquent and intensely passionate description of love as the most powerful emotion on earth:

For love is fierce as death,
Passion is mighty as Sheol;
Its darts are darts of fire,
A blazing flame. . . .
Great seas cannot extinguish love,
No river can sweep it away.

The Song of Songs exalts love, desire, intimacy, and joy. The lovers' air of generosity and abandon is striking. They are open to one another without equivocation or ambivalence. They express their feelings freely, with wholesomeness and lack of inhibition. At times they speak directly to each other; at other times they talk about each other. Some songs describe dreams, others daydreams or fantasies. The lovers compete to express their admiration and delight in each other. Their declarations have the ring of youthful sincerity and fresh enthusiasm rather than sophisticated, practiced flattery. The lovers feel equal and self-confident; they take turns becoming the pursuer and the pursued. The poetic descriptions of genuine female eroticism, which is absent from the rest of the scriptures, legitimize it as worthwhile in its own right.

The Song of Songs is permeated with a love for the land of Israel, showing a deep familiarity with her geographical locations, her seasons, and her flora and fauna. The woman says of herself, "I am the rose of Sharon," referring to the flower named for the plain along the Mediterranean coast. Ein Gedi (on the shores of the Dead Sea) and the Tower of David in Jerusalem are also mentioned. The lovers make repeated references to Jerusalem, the capital ("You are beautiful, my darling, comely as Jerusalem"). The woman extols her lover's grace in exaggerated terms: "He is as majestic as Lebanon," the tallest mountain in the land. The lover responds to her with further natural and geographical imagery: "Your hair is like a flock of goats streaming down from Gilead" (in northern Israel).

The setting is the eternal Mediterranean, lush with native date palms, lilies, roses, fig trees, cypresses, pomegranates, apples, and the occasional pair of gazelles. The fruits are erotic symbols reminiscent of the "fruit" in the Garden of Eden. The lovers meet outdoors and at night in the luxuriant warmth of a subtropical climate.

. . .

THE PREVAILING THEORY IS THAT many of the poems were passed down orally over the centuries and that the collection was edited into its present form around the third century BCE. For a long time King Solomon was credited with authoring the Song of Songs in addition to the books of Proverbs and Ecclesiastes. This attribution may have stemmed from his being thought of as the lover of a thousand women and therefore assumed to be adept at wooing the fairer sex. The woman's name, Shulamite, also gives some credence to the Solomon theory because the name shares a root, *shalem*, with the name of Solomon's capital, Jerusalem, Yerushalayim in Hebrew. Some of the poems refer to Solomon and his wealth, and some merely cite "my king." Yet Shulamite is dismissive of wealth, asserting that

> *If a man tried to buy love*
> *With all the wealth of his house,*
> *He would be despised.*

But Shulamite does not mindlessly celebrate sensual love. She suggests that there is an optimum time for physical love too.

> *His left hand beneath my head,*
> *His right arm holding me close.*

> *Daughters of Jerusalem, swear to me*
> *That you will never awaken love*
> *Until it is ripe.*

Not surprisingly, some suggest that a woman wrote the Song of Songs. Many more verses are ascribed to women than to men, and we know more about Shulamite's personality than that of her lover. She is bold and fearless, and it is she who takes the initiative in the relationship. The numerous dreams relate to the Shulamite's inner life, with which the poet is familiar. The Song of Songs begins and ends with the woman's voice. We may never know if the author was a woman, but we do know that a woman's erotic longings have been explored here with depth and understanding.

GOD IS NEVER MENTIONED IN the eight chapters of the poems. Their inclusion in a sacred book seemed inappropriate and had been a topic of intense rabbinical debate. The great Rabbi Akiva, born in about 50 CE, developed a brilliant solution to this anomaly. He suggested that the love between the couple is an allegory of God's love for the people of Israel and that the pair's longings for each other represented mankind's overwhelming spiritual yearning for God's love. It is worth noting that Rabbi Akiva's marriage was particularly happy, following a romantic courtship. His interpretation satisfied the rabbis charged with editing the Bible into its ultimate form and saved this beautiful piece of literature from oblivion. Early Christianity found similar comfort, regarding the poems as an allegory of Jesus' love and closeness to the Church.

The romanticism of the Songs of Songs' eroticism contrasts starkly with the blatant sexuality of the commercial media, with their drumbeat of advertisements advising that the most important motivation for human activity is sexual attraction and that purchasing a certain brand of beer, deodorant, or car will make us more desirable and therefore happy. Now the Internet inundates us with offers for hard-core pornography, usually humiliating and denigrating to women. Sexual images are insinuated into children's television programs and conveyed through crude innuendo as well as in the explicit imagery of music videos, video games, billboards, and movies. Our culture eroticizes children early and inappropriately. By the time young people are mature enough to handle the emotional and physical realities of a sexual relationship, they have been on fast forward for too long and skipped the necessary stages of normal adolescent maturation. As Dr. Willard Gaylin, in his book *On Being and Becoming Human*, has observed, "these days it is easier for many young people to go to bed with one another than to form trusting and intimate relationships. It is easier for them to expose their genitals to a stranger than to expose their feelings."

We talk more about the how-to of sex than any other generation, yet I fear we know less. We exaggerate the importance of technique over feelings and imagination. We refer to "having sex" as though sex were a commodity, whereas the older expression, "making love," emphasizes the journey and the emotional closeness.

Now that we have broken through the crass ceiling, I wonder if we can ever recapture the wholesomeness and unstudied joy of the lovers in the Song of Songs. What, in fact, do these ancient love poems have to do with us?

The poems return us to equality between the sexes, the give-and-take that sustains the core of true intimacy, tenderness, and passion. Erotica does not objectify or commercialize the male-female relationship, while in the long run, pornography turns the dynamics between two people into a crude exercise that fully satisfies neither women nor men. What we find erotic in the poems is the emphasis on imagination and the throbbing sense of yearning for intimacy, safety, and closeness, conditions that delight women and will inevitably increase the pleasure of their partners.

In the first story of the Bible, set in the Garden of Eden, the archetypical Adam and Eve experience the universal passage into sexual awakening and love. In the stories that follow, the biblical characters use or abuse God's gift of desire and sex. In the Song of Songs, we find that the two lovers have once again created a Garden of Eden for themselves.

Just as *Hamlet* is never as rich in Hebrew as it is in English, so the Songs are more evocative in their original language—a sufficient reason in itself to study Hebrew. Readers are encouraged to read the entire Song of Songs to themselves, share it with their lovers, read it for the beauty of the language and find their own interpretations of its hidden meanings. So long as they do the Songs will never die.

CONCLUSION

⁂

THE SEVENTEEN WOMEN PORTRAYED IN this book all played decisive roles during the two-thousand-year history chronicled in the Hebrew Bible. My approach to the biblical stories has been personal, based on a lifetime of teaching and studying the commentaries, which were written over hundreds of years, as well as my life experiences as wife, mother, psychotherapist, and teacher.

What I find particularly intriguing about the women is that most of them circumvent male authority in a patriarchal society, and some even subvert it. Even more remarkable is the fact that the women, other than Jezebel, are never punished for their unconventional conduct. On the contrary, the biblical scribes treat the women with deep sympathy, and are sensitive to their plight, and all of them, with the exception of the ruthless and grasping Jezebel, are rewarded for their boldness.

Most of the women defy male authority when it is unjust or does not answer their needs or those of their family or their people. They belong to a patriarchal society in which men hold all visible power, and their options are few and stark. Given these circumstances, the women challenge, they seduce, and they trick. They take risks, and some, such as Queen Esther and Judah's daughter-in-law Tamar, are prepared to stake their lives on the outcome. Both Tamar and Ruth are widows who would be doomed to a life of poverty and anonymity but for the initiative they take in devising careful plans of sexual seduction. Not only do the men respond, but the descendants of their acts of seduction become progenitors of the House of David generations later. Both women are rewarded for the risk they take to ensure the survival of the family.

In selecting the women, I was drawn to their vulnerabilities as much as to their strengths. Like the timeless heroines of the Hebrew Bible, we too struggle to love, to parent, to succeed in relationships, and to make our way through the labyrinth of a dangerous world. In each of the stories women are the protagonists around whom the action revolves.

The young Eve speaks to me with her optimism as she leaves the Garden of Eden with her man to start adult life in the real and imperfect world. My heart aches for Sarah, who, with the best of intentions, puts another woman into the bed of her husband, Abraham, to produce the son she cannot conceive. I admire Rebecca's tragic, divisive, but courageous choice, made in the long-term interests of an entire people. A fearless woman, she questions the law of primogeniture when it stands in the way of the survival of the Covenant. I am delighted by Abigail's persuasive charm, artfully contrived to please and tame the young future king of Israel, and in the process save herself and her household from bloodshed. And my imagination is captured by the exotic, entrepreneurial Queen of Sheba. The illicit and passionate love affair between David and Bathsheba, although it matures into a long-term marriage, raises serious and troubling universal issues. These are but a few of the compelling stories of the women of the Bible whose lives resonate with us today.

NOW THAT WOMEN HAVE BEGUN studying the biblical text in substantial numbers, feminist scholars and others have begun writing much about women in the Bible. Some of them feature fighters like Deborah, the biblical Joan of Arc, who leads the Israelites in battle, and the midwives Puah and Shifrah, who save Hebrew male babies despite Pharaoh's edict to drown them in the Nile. Another heroine is the prostitute Rahab, who risks her life to help Joshua's spies escape from Jericho. While the Bible recounts the actions for which these heroines are remembered, it tells us nothing about their interior lives and processes of decision and thus gives few clues how we can emulate them today.

Except for Delilah and Jezebel, I chose those women with whom I am able to identify and who interact with the men in their lives—with surprising results. These intelligent, brave women dare and take the initiative. They are assertive, unwilling to be passive victims in the face of overwhelming circumstances. They are not looking for ways to raise their self-esteem, nor are their lives directed by a need to "feel good" or "feel comfortable." What keeps them going despite adverse circumstances is the power of a purpose-driven life and an all-embracing faith—values that demand both a long-term view of history and a decisive, resourceful approach to the immediate present. One is hard put to find in them a hint of alienation, cynicism, or ennui; on the contrary, they convey a can-do approach to life as they prevail, overcome, and refuse to bow in the face of overwhelming odds. In making their choices these most heroic of women are guided by the long-term interests of their families and people. They make and execute their imperfect decisions to the best of their abilities, and they are willing to acknowledge and live with the consequences of their actions—the essential meaning of the responsibility and accountability that accompanies free will, God's greatest gift to humans.

THE LEGAL STATUS OF BIBLICAL women is unequal to the status of men. Women are second-class citizens living under the authority of the head of their family, usually their fathers or husbands. And yet, surprisingly enough, the women in these stories are neither downtrodden nor crushed by stern, brutal patriarchs. Within the family the women wield enormous power. When they see their family or their tribe in danger, and the men fail to act, women fill the vacuum, taking the risks and assuming responsibilities for the destiny of their people. The narrative also suggests that women, with their limited legal status, are a metaphor for all minorities struggling to make their voices heard. The women's situation is analogous to that of the Israelites, a tough small people set amongst more powerful pagan cultures.

In biblical times polygamy was practiced widely. Yet each polygamous family portrayed in the Bible is unhappy. (Each is unhappy in its own way, as Tolstoy wrote many centuries later.) Whether the problem is the rivalry between Rachel and Leah, the two sisters married to Jacob, or between Hannah and Peninnah, both married to Elkanah, or the conflicting demands by David's many wives and their feuding children, the biblical authors subtly point out the disadvantages of a polygamous marriage. In contrast, Sarah and Abraham form a distinctly monogamous marriage within a polygamous culture, as do Rebecca and Isaac. In the Garden of Eden too we have one woman and one man. The narrative makes clear that an intense relationship between husband and wife in a polygamous marriage is nearly impossible. The presence of multiple, contending wives dilutes all the relationships within the family unit. The Bible strongly implies that polygamy does not work and that monogamy is a preferable structure. The intensely committed personal and loving relationship between one male and one female parallels the intensely committed relationship between one human and God.

In the Hebrew Bible, sexuality is by no means a secret, sinful, or forbidden subject. Instead sex is discussed with remarkable openness and with no trace of prudishness. We are carried away by the beautifully written Song of Songs, as it celebrates in explicit terms the sensual love between Shulamite and her lover. The Bible regards sexuality as the Creator's gift, integral to all human life, to be used as a tool for strengthening the bonds of intimacy, trust, companionship, responsibility and commitment.

On the other hand, sexuality can also be abusive and selfish. The Bible's unvarnished realism does not spare us this aspect of human ambivalence. The Israelite hero Samson becomes addicted to Delilah's sexual favors. She hands him over to her people, Israel's enemies, who blind, torture, and imprison him. The worst example of sex as a destructive force is Amnon's inexorable plot to rape his virgin half sister Tamar, King David's beautiful daughter. She staggers out of his house, her life forever ruined.

The Bible instructs even as it entertains. It does not whitewash any aspect of human psychology or conduct. It draws the reader in by exposing its protagonists' feet of clay. No one is spared critical comment or the depiction of unflattering weaknesses—and no one is above the law. The women, like their men, are responsible for their actions and the consequences. The women and the men are neither saints nor sinners, and interestingly enough, their actions are treated with equal candor.

The stories of the women in the Hebrew Bible offer us a prism through which to consider our own lives. After all, human nature has not changed one iota since the day Eve, the first in the gallery of enterprising women, questions the rules in the Garden of Eden in response to her God-given drive to acquire knowledge and to create new life. The outcome is the first exercise of free choice and the first lesson in personal responsibility and morality.

The biblical chroniclers observe human nature carefully as they probe complex conflicts and individual lives. No one said life would be easy; it isn't. Human beings are too complicated and want too many conflicting things at the same time, such as head-whirling romance and stable, supportive love, immediate gratification and long-term satisfaction. The Bible never stoops to simplify, and therein lies its power, its humanity, its timelessness. For this I am eternally grateful.

In his book *God in Search of Man* (1955), Abraham Joshua Heschel writes, "Among the many things that religious tradition holds in store for us is a legacy of wonder." In these words I hear an echo of the biblical narrators who, thousands of years earlier, offered a similar observation in the book of Proverbs, attributed to King Solomon:

> *There are three things which are too wonderful for me,*
> *Yea, four which I know not:*
> *The way of an eagle in the air;*
> *The way of a serpent upon a rock.*
> *The way of a ship in the midst of the sea;*
> *And the way of a man with a woman.*

After studying the Hebrew Bible, contemporary readers may wish to append a final line to the poem:

> *And the way of a woman with a man.*

ACKNOWLEDGMENTS

This book is the end product of the journey that began in my child-hood with lively discussions at my parents' supper table and the profoundly stimulating discussions with my learned teachers at the Reali School in Haifa Israel. Each in turn filled me with love, wonder, respect and awe for the eternal Book. The journey continues.

My earliest thanks go to Gail Ross, my book agent, who encouraged me and got me started writing on Biblical subjects. To Jonathan Burnham, the president of Miramax Books, who is both demanding and tough, polite and solicitous. To Susan Mercandetti, who believed in the book and in me from the very start. To the Miramax team—Kathy Schneider, Publisher; Claire Mc Kinney,

Director of Publicity; Kristin Powers, Director of Production; the efficient and capable Caroline Clayton; Barrie Gordon; Jamie Horn— thank you.

To Cheryl Silver and Charles Fenyvesi, my profound thanks for their work, their suggestions, contributions and even humor— they were invaluable.

To Senator Arlen Specter, who hosted my weekly Bible study group for senators from both sides of the aisle, who exposed me to the unchanging character of the tensions between ethics and power; to Bill Moyers' *Genesis a Living Conversation*; to my Friday morning Bible seminars—my thanks. I am still feasting on the analysis and readings of the Biblical text that I derived from them all.

To those who offered me ideas and insights, companionship and support, my profound thanks: Ingeborg Hydle Baugh, Leslie Cashen, Susan Dalsimer, Barbara Davis, Marjorie Elfin, Nitza Ben-Elissar, Peter Ford, Robbie Hare, Joshua Horwitz, Tamara Kemp, Jenna Land, Susan Nash, Dr. Sheila Rogovin, Helene Rosenblatt, Richard Rosenblatt, Laurene Sherlock, Carol Shookhoff, Kena Shoval, Anna Saint John, Dr. David Trachtenberg, Jack Valenti, Howard Yoon. Last but not least, I am grateful to my husband, Peter, who is always my toughest critic and staunchest supporter.